MORE THAN WORDS

More than Words

A Memoir of a Writing Life

JERRY APPS

Wisconsin Historical Society Press

Published by the Wisconsin Historical Society Press
Publishers since 1855

The Wisconsin Historical Society helps people connect to the past by collecting, preserving, and sharing stories. Founded in 1846, the Society is one of the nation's finest historical institutions.
Join the Wisconsin Historical Society: wisconsinhistory.org/membership

Printed in Canada
Typesetting by Wendy Holdman
26 25 24 23 22   1 2 3 4 5

Library of Congress Cataloging-in-Publication Data

Names: Apps, Jerold W., 1934– author.
Title: More than words : a memoir of a writing life / Jerry Apps.
Description: [Madison, Wisconsin] : Wisconsin Historical Society Press, [2022] | Includes bibliographical references.
Identifiers: LCCN 2021060208 (print) | LCCN 2021060209 (e-book) | ISBN 9780870209970 (hardcover) | ISBN 9780870209987 (epub)
Subjects: LCSH: Apps, Jerold W., 1934– | Authors, American—20th Century—Biography. | College teachers—Wisconsin—Biography. | Authorship. | Wisconsin—Biography.
Classification: LCC PS3601.P67 Z46 2022 (print) | LCC PS3601.P67 (e-book) | DDC 813/.6 [B]—dc23/eng/20220419
LC record available at https://lccn.loc.gov/2021060208
LC ebook record available at https://lccn.loc.gov/2021060209

♾ The paper used in this publication meets the minimum requirements of the American National Standard for Information Sciences—Permanence of Paper for Printed Library Materials, ANSI Z39.48-1992.

For Ruth, my in-house editor

Contents

Preface

On January 12, 1996, I wrote in my journal: "Yesterday was a notable day. My last day of work at the University of Wisconsin–Madison. I turned in my keys to Pam, head secretary for the Department of Continuing and Vocational Education. One marked 'OD' for outside door to the Teacher Education Building, one marked 264 for the outer office, and one marked 10 for my private office. This was the first day since 1956 that I have not worked for someone else."

My graduate students were not happy that I was leaving. It is never easy for a student to switch major advisors in the middle of a graduate program. But I was committed to my decision to take early retirement from the university and write full-time—despite the advice of my long-time writing mentor, Robert Gard, who had once told me, "Keep your day job, Jerry. Income from writing is terribly unpredictable."

On the day I turned in my keys, I was sixty-one years old. According to a fellow professor in my department, I was at the peak of my academic career. "Why in the world would you want to leave now?" he asked. "You will lose a bunch of retirement money!" Retirement income was based on the number of years taught and the average of your highest three years' salaries. I could have taught for another nine years, maybe more. I told him, "I want time to do research, write, and teach."

"But that's what you are supposed to be doing now," he said, a perplexed look on his face.

I liked teaching and had especially enjoyed my students, who challenged me with questions I couldn't always answer and showed me new perspectives I had never considered. But for the past several years, I explained, I had spent the majority of my time not teaching classes, researching, or writing, but on administrative work—untold hours in meetings of one kind or another, more hours dealing with personnel problems, and still more hours juggling budgets. I had just completed four years as director of the National Extension Leadership Development Program; it had been a good experience, but it, too, had kept me away from what I most wanted to do. And before directing the leadership program, I had served seven years as department chair, working through budget cuts, realignments, and changes in focus on top of the everyday tasks of managing a large university department.

Ruth and I talked a good deal about the possibility of me turning to full-time writing. By that time, our three children had graduated from college and were well into their chosen careers. (In 1996, Susan was thirty-four, Steve thirty-three, and Jeff thirty-two.) We added up our household expenses, and we decided that we could make it, as long as my writing brought in some income. I would earn my teacher's pension and continue to teach writing courses at the School of the Arts in Rhinelander and at The Clearing in Door County. And I looked forward to a little more income when I reached sixty-five and would begin to collect Social Security.

Ruth agreed to continue serving as my first reader and editor—and as bookseller when we were on the road. I asked the children for their help as well. Steve, at the time a staff photographer for the *Wisconsin State Journal* with a bachelor's degree in mass communications, and his partner, Natasha, with a journalism degree, agreed to read my draft material. Sue, an elementary teacher with a master's degree in reading, signed on too, as did Jeff, an investment counselor. I was truly blessed to have my entire family's support of my writing.

I set up a modest writing office in a basement room where we had once stored our storm windows. I fashioned a desk by attaching a leg to each corner of an old door. The space was small, with no windows, but it worked. I could write without interruption until noon—although I did discover that stopping at ten each morning for a second cup of coffee was a nice break, a habit I continue to this day. (My Norwegian in-laws always stopped whatever they were doing for morning coffee. My German relatives never did that.)

It was official. After many years of thinking about taking the leap, I was now a full-time writer. But in one way or another, I had been on the writing path for nearly my entire life.

1 Why a Writer?

I grew up among storytellers, my father being one of the best. Storytelling was a popular pastime in those years before television, and the characters and goings-on in our small farming community seemed to be an endless source of stories—stories told at silo-filling, threshing, and wood-sawing bees and behind the woodstove in the back of Hotz's Hardware on a winter Saturday night, where my dad and I waited for my mother and twin brothers while they traded eggs for groceries at the Wild Rose Mercantile. I heard stories of winters past, when the snow piled higher and the thermometer dipped lower than anyone today could imagine. I heard stories of huge fish caught and ten-point bucks bagged. Some of the stories were funny, some sad, some filled with bits of country wisdom or important life lessons, and some, as my dad once told me, "stretching the truth a bit."

In the time before electricity came to the countryside, our battery-operated radio was our main connection to the outside world. Standing on its little table in the kitchen, our Philco was another source of stories. As a kid, I listened to what my mother dubbed "Jerold's stories"—fifteen-minute-long serials that aired Monday

I learned from a young age that stories were an important part of life in our rural community.

through Friday. My favorites were *The Lone Ranger, Captain Midnight, Terry and the Pirates*, and *Jack Armstrong*. The stories were filled with excitement, bravery, strong characters, and lots of suspense to keep me listening.

When I was fourteen or so, I was old enough to work on a threshing crew, going from farm to farm to help neighbors with the grain harvest. After an enormous threshing meal, the crew would gather under a tree, rest, and tell stories. I mostly listened, but I was learning the power of stories to entertain and to bring people together.

The first writing I remember doing was in second or third grade at the one-room country school my brothers and I attended, Chain O' Lake School. Every year before school started, my mother would take me to the drugstore in Wild Rose and buy me a new five-cent lined tablet, two No. 2 lead pencils, and a small box of crayons. Back at home, my dad sharpened the pencils with his jackknife. On the first day of school, I headed down our dusty country road with my new school supplies and the excitement that came with each new school year.

The various teachers we had over the years insisted that my fellow students and I learn how to write cursive, as they called it (or longhand, as we called it). Our model was Spenserian script, examples of which were strung above the blackboards on the front wall of the schoolroom. Being a bit headstrong, I could see no sense practicing the swigs and swags that made up this elegant cursive form. As soon as I was able to read, I could usually be found with my nose in a book while my fellow students were practicing writing longhand.

It was in that little school that I learned how to spell, how to tell a subject from a predicate, where to put an adjective or an adverb in a sentence, and the other basics of writing—although at the time, becoming a writer was the furthest thing from my mind. I also learned how to learn on my own, digging for answers to my unending questions about things small and large, as the teacher had limited time to spend with each student.

My family had few books at home, so it was also at Chain O' Lake School that I developed my love for books. The school library was tiny, three or four short shelves nailed to the north wall near the woodstove. By the time I reached sixth grade, I had read every book in the school's limited collection, even the thick ones like *Uncle Tom's Cabin*.

Once I had exhausted the school library's collection, I thought I was out of luck. In those days, the Wild Rose

The fundamentals I learned at our one-room country school made me a lifelong reader and writer.

public library would not lend books to kids who lived outside the village. Luckily, Arnol Roberts, owner of the Wild Rose Mercantile, knew about my love for books. In the store basement—where you could buy everything from four-buckle barn boots to groceries—Mr. Roberts offered a small assortment of hardcover books, none priced more than forty-nine cents. While my mother was busy grocery shopping, Mr. Roberts would take me down to his book collection and recommend books for me to buy. I saved the money I earned picking cucumbers, potatoes, and green beans and used it to buy books. I still have several of them in my home library today: *Swiss Family Robinson*, *Treasure Island*, *The Black Arrow*, and others.

It was during my eighth-grade year, in 1947, that I contracted polio. During the several months that I was recovering at home, I began keeping a diary—the first in a journaling practice that I continue to this day. Polio and its aftermath prevented me from participating in sports at Wild Rose High School, and one of my teachers suggested I enroll in a typing class. On the first day, I found myself—the only boy in the class—sitting in front of a formidable-looking L. C. Smith manual typewriter. At the time I had seen a typewriter only once or twice and had never given any thought to how to operate one. One of the first questions I asked our teacher, Mr. Harvey, was, "Why are the letters not in the order of the alphabet?" He went into a long explanation about how the letters were placed that way so the typewriter keys wouldn't jam. I didn't understand his answer, but some of my classmates were looking at me funny, and I decided to keep my mouth shut and see if I could learn how to operate the strange-looking machine. After all, I thought, I can drive a Farmall H Tractor, and it is a lot more complicated than this typewriter.

Soon Mr. Harvey had us typing the sentence "The quick brown fox jumps over the lazy dog." It made no sense to me at all. The last thing our farm dog would do was allow a fox to jump over her. But as instructed, I began to punch the typewriter keys. And I discovered that I used every key on the keyboard—the entire alphabet—to create those words. I smiled. The sentence was pretty clever, I had to admit.

Anyone who has ever typed on a manual typewriter knows that you've got to do more than softly touch the keys—you've got to strike them with some intensity. Every finger has to do its share. Fortunately, I had strong fingers, as one of my chores at home was milking cows by hand. Some of the girls in the class were having problems typing the "a" on one end of keyboard and the ";" on the other end. Weak pinkie fingers. No problem for me.

I found I liked the class. When I got to the end of a line and the little bell rang, I pushed a lever, the carriage returned, and I started another line. It was almost magical to see words appearing on a sheet of paper in front of me. The sound of letters striking paper was pleasant. Besides all that, I could read what I had typed—everyone could read it! My handwriting was next to impossible to read.

It turned out that those of us in the typing class were also on the school's newspaper staff, typing up each issue of the *Rosebud* before it was printed on a hectograph machine. I became a reporter, assistant editor, and then editor. It was fun digging for a story, typing it up, and seeing it appear in print in the *Rosebud*. I became hooked on writing, and I've never gotten over it.

In the fall of 1951, I enrolled in the College of Agriculture at the University of Wisconsin–Madison on a scholarship. Like all freshmen, I was required to take English 1A and English 1B. I looked forward to those two courses—but was sadly disappointed when my English professors didn't care for my writing and gave me Cs. I had been valedictorian of my high school senior class and was not accustomed to receiving Cs. As a result of those disappointments, the only writing I did throughout college was the required term papers and essays. It was one of my early low points and nearly a devastating blow to any future writing career. When I graduated from the UW–Madison with honors in 1955, I had put any thoughts of creative writing on hold, if not abandoned them entirely.

2 First Professional Writing

After earning my bachelor's degree in 1955 and completing my military service in 1956, I enrolled in graduate school at the University of Wisconsin and completed a master's degree in 1957. With my first postcollege job, as the UW College of Agriculture extension agent in Green Lake, Wisconsin, I quickly found myself with my first professional writing assignments. Along with meeting with farm families and 4-H leaders and helping organize the Green Lake County Fair, I was responsible for writing a weekly column for the local newspaper, the *Berlin Journal*. Most of my columns consisted of journalistic reports on the activities of the county 4-H clubs and could not be classified as creative writing. But I did manage to slip personal-interest stories into many of them. I wrote about a young 4-H member telling me how much fun he had at the county fair, about another member describing the challenges of teaching her calf how to lead, and others.

After two and half years in Green Lake, I took a job as extension agent for Brown County and moved to Green Bay. Now I was writing two columns a week, one for the *Green Bay Press-Gazette* and the other for the county's weekly newspapers. Ray Pagel, farm editor for the *Press-Gazette*, was an old-school journalist who, with red pencil in hand, reworked every column I wrote for his paper. At first I was put off by the many red marks on my columns, but I realized he was teaching me how to be a better writer. I had never taken a university course in journalism and was learning on the job. Gruff and never bending, Ray Pagel was a good teacher. He must have seen some potential in my writing. My time with the *Press-Gazette* included many high points, when my columns passed muster with Pagel, and low points, when they didn't.

In 1962, with Ruth and baby Sue, I moved from Green Bay to Madison, where I had been hired as the publications editor for the College of Agriculture's state 4-H office. My staff consisted of a copyeditor and a secretary. Our task: creating thousands of copies of bulletins for 4-H members throughout the state. The topics ranged from cooking and baking to feeding a dairy calf and basic carpentry skills, and the text was written by College of Agriculture professors. My job was to help the professors—who of course were accustomed to writing for academic audiences—to write for young people ages ten to twenty-one. During the two and half years I spent in that job helping others revise their writing, I had neither the time nor the energy to do any writing of my own. But I was learning on the job how to edit. I also enrolled in a university course on bulletin editing. The editing skills I learned then have served me well over the years.

In 1964, I left editing bulletins for a position as assistant professor in the College of Agriculture. Again I had little time for my own writing, as I began full-time teaching along with doing research and writing academic articles for publication. In order to advance my career at

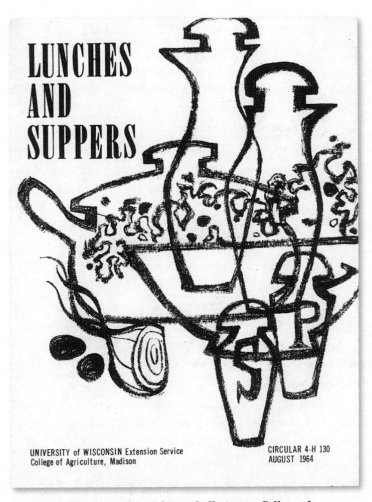

Lunches and Suppers was one of many bulletins my College of Agriculture publications team created for 4-H members.

the university I would need a PhD, and in 1964 I enrolled in a graduate program for part-time study. Now there was no time at all for creative writing, as I was teaching full-time and studying part-time, although I did occasionally sneak a story into the papers I was required to write for my graduate courses.

In the 1960s, University of Wisconsin–Madison PhD programs required candidates to spend at least one year committed to full-time study and research. For me that year was 1966: twelve months devoted to studying, reading, thinking, and eventually writing my dissertation (a mostly dry piece of academic writing written in third person throughout and including such memorable phrases as "This researcher, upon examining all dimensions of the research, concludes that . . ." In keeping with the academic approach, my major professor had instructed me never to write in the first person.)

While I was meant to be focusing on academic writing, I yearned to write for a general audience. Thoughts of freelance writing returned. I signed up for a noncredit evening course for potential freelance writers taught by Al Nelson, a professional writer from Delafield, Wisconsin. Nelson taught us how to write query letters to potential publishers and create a piece of writing that could be easily read by "ordinary" people, not just academics.

As I slogged through the required chapters of my dissertation, I began writing articles and short stories for publication, including a weekly column called Outdoor Notebook for the Waushara Argus, a weekly newspaper published in Wautoma, Wisconsin. Now, for the first time, I was able to put into practice what I had learned from Ray Pagel in Green Bay, from my years working as a UW publications editor, and from writing instructor Al Nelson. Soon several other newspapers in central Wisconsin had picked up Outdoor Notebook. Some of the columns were good, and some were awful, but every one was published. Since my days as a 4-H member, I have believed in the importance of learning by doing. The ten years I spent writing Outdoor Notebook served as a writing apprenticeship.

The Country Is Its Own Teacher

OUTDOOR NOTEBOOK
By Jerry Apps

Kids and the country go together well. That really isn't news to anybody. Except it really impressed me the days we were vacationing at Roshara. Our kids are city kids. They know about blocks, and sidewalks, and traffic. These they take for granted and have made a part of their lives.

So the country is new to them, a whole new set of experiences. There are no sidewalks at Roshara. A block is four miles around, and traffic-- well every time a car goes by the farm we stretch our necks to see if we know who it is.

But there are much greater differences than the obvious. Take the day we were walking in the far corner of Roshara where there's a little woodlot-- maybe a couple acres of black oak trees and some gray dogwood and hazel brush. Of course there's much more if you stop and look. That day we were doing lots of stopping and looking.

Susie saw it first. "What is it?" she asked as she pointed to the mound of dirt, punched full of holes on top and crawling with ants.

"It's an ant hill, Sue. Let's watch it for awhile," I suggested. Sue and Jeff wanted to get as close as they could and before they were aware, ants were crawling over their shoes and then on their bare legs.

"Dad, dad, there're on me!" Sue screamed. Jeff didn't say anything, he just jumped up and down and shook all over. I helped brush off the ants and then we sat down and talked about the ant hill, the society ants have, how they store food, and so on.

I'm sure both Sue and Jeff had read about ant hills in their school books, but until now an ant hill was some kind of abstract thing existing only on the dead pages of a book. Now they were learning about ant hills, by watching, by listening, and by feeling. The experience was real, alive to them. It just happened, it wasn't planned yet the children learned.

That same afternoon the kids were walking to the neighbors for some drinking water -- our well water is still questionable for drinking. On the driveway they found a small turtle -- and we nearly didn't get the water. The three of them spent most of the afternoon playing with the turtle. (They did stop long enough -- with some encouragement -- to bring back the jugs.)

What's so fascinating about a turtle? One lived in their aquarium at school. But this turtle was different. Here was a turtle all by itself, on the way to the pond I suppose, and the kids could pick it up and look at it. They could feel the turtle's leathery shell and watch its head slip in and out.

EXCITING DISCOVERY–It was only a little turtle, yet the kids were fascinated and played most of an afternoon with it.

They put the turtle in a pan with a stone and some water and watched it. They saw how it breathed, saw what it would do when turned on its back -- in a split second it was uprighted.

And then they had to make some decisions. What to do with the turtle? Keep it as a pet? They liked that idea. But I suggested we had no suitable place. Let it go? "But it's so much fun to play with," they cried.

The decision was finally made, they carried the turtle to the pond.

"He was goin' that way anyway," Jeff said. "This way he got there quicker."

You can't really teach kids about the country, you can only bring kids and the country together. The teaching will take care of itself.

My Outdoor Notebook column was a space to explore subjects I care about, such as nature and our connection to the land. In the story above, I described my children's encounter with a turtle.

I was paid five dollars for each column, and therefore 1966 was the year I began calling myself a professional writer. It also marked the beginning of a dual career— full-time as a university professor and part-time as a freelance writer, an arrangement I would continue until 1996.

When I began freelancing, fledgling writers like me could often find a publishing opportunity in their home-town papers. Many local papers were looking for community histories—stories about notable people, historic buildings and places, and so on. Magazines were popular then too, and many of them, especially the regional ones, accepted freelance material. The pay wasn't much, usually five or ten dollars a story, but the work was a way to gain practical experience as a writer.

I wasn't content with merely writing for the *Waushara Argus*, however; I wanted national success. Starting in 1966, I wrote articles on a variety of topics and sent them off to major national publishers such as *Reader's Digest*, the *New Yorker*, and the *Atlantic*. I wrote about everything from how pipe smoking enhances thinking (it doesn't) to how to make a bluebird house out of a coffee can (not a great idea) and many other articles of similar import. Every one of those early submissions resulted in a rejection. When a manuscript was mailed back to me, I removed it from the stamped, self-addressed envelope that I had included with my original submission and stuffed it in another envelope addressed to another publisher, along with another self-addressed and stamped envelope. I did this for a half dozen years with no success other than my weekly columns. Some days I wondered if I should have taken up woodworking, model building, furniture refurnishing, or just about anything other than writing. Several of my friends and relatives saw my writing as a hobby—but I wanted it to be more than that.

I stopped writing my weekly column for the *Waushara Argus* after ten years, in 1976. I was ready to leave column writing behind and concentrate on other publishing opportunities. It would take thirty-seven years, but eventually I would once again write newspaper columns. In the meantime, I thought it would be a fun new challenge to write a book.

3 *The Land Still Lives*

By 1968, I had been writing my Outdoor Notebook column for two years, and from the comments and letters
received, readers appeared to enjoy it. In many of the
columns I described my family's experiences at Roshara,
the abandoned, rundown farm in Waushara County that
Ruth and I had bought in 1966. We were working to re-
store the farm as close as possible to what it had been in
1867, when Civil War veteran Tom Stewart homesteaded
the land, and in Outdoor Notebook I recounted stories
of spending time with the family on this land, where we
transformed a 1912 granary into a cabin, planted trees
and put up bluebird houses, and enjoyed the sunsets,
the quiet evenings, and the sound of the whip-poor-will
calling its name as we fell asleep. The column provided
me the opportunity to explore many topics that interested me: nature, the environment, history, and our
connection to the land.

I wondered whether a collection of Outdoor Notebook columns might make a good book. I gathered
twenty-five of what I thought were examples of my best
writing to show to Robert Gard, a faculty member in my
department at the university and author of several books

about Wisconsin. With his friend L. G. Sorden he ran a small publishing company called Wisconsin House that published three or four books a year. Wisconsin House published several of Gard's books, including *Down in the Valleys*, *The Only Place I Live*, and *This Is Wisconsin*, along with works by other notable Wisconsin writers, including Jerry Minnich and Sara Rath.

I met with Bob one day, clutching several of my columns, and asked him if he would take a look. A week or so later I met with him again. He said the columns were interesting, but he suggested I use the content of my columns as the basis for a book, rather than simply collecting them in book form. I agreed. On July 2, 1970, I received a contract from Wisconsin House for *The Land Still Lives* stipulating that I should "deliver to the Publisher on or before July 15, 1970, a complete manuscript copy of the work, of approximately 40,000 words in length, in its final revised form, including all drawings, charts, designs and illustrations which are to be included in the text."

According to the contract, I would earn royalties on books sold as follows: "On all copies of the work in regular trade edition sold by the publisher in the United States at discounts less than forty-eight per cent (48%) from the catalogue price, a royalty computed on the catalogue price as follows: 8% for the first 2,000 copies sold. Thereafter 10%. Royalty after 10,000 copies sold to be negotiated with the author." The book's price was set at $5.95. My royalty for the first two thousand copies sold would be 47.8 cents per book.

The first printing of *The Land Still Lives* was three thousand copies. As soon as the book came out, I began to do book signings in Madison at such places as the University Book Store and Prange's department store and in my hometown of Wild Rose at the Patterson Memorial Library.

Like my Outdoor Notebook column, writing *The Land Still Lives* provided me an outlet for exploring topics that matter to me. In the book's prologue, I wrote:

Ruthie and I are interested in Roshara not as an economic venture, but as a place to get acquainted with the outdoors, to develop a relationship with nature and all its mystery and wonder. Having both grown up on farms in Wisconsin, we now want to offer the same experience to our three children. . . .

Our feelings toward Roshara and what it has to offer are deep and continuing. We feel there comes a time when every person asks, what is my life all about? Am I making it all it could be? Am I providing my children with opportunities that will help them seek quality in their lives?

We search out answers as we roam Roshara's hills, explore its woodlots, and walk by its pond. The questions prompt us to study Roshara's history and learn of its owners before us, people who got to know this land intimately and to love it.

Communing with the outdoors, on nature's terms, gives us a feeling of inward satisfaction and peace of mind. We seek to understand, to relate to present and past, to gain a feeling for the land. Our plan is not to change the land, not to convert it to some other man's image of what it should be.

We seek only to be a part of what is happening at Roshara. We do not want to dominate. We search for solitude, freedom, and beauty, and with only enough environmental change to enable us to live there. We seek the opportunity to dream, to look at our lives and find meaning. Roshara is where we can do this.

I couldn't have known it at the time, but *The Land Still Lives* was the first of many books I would write that combine my interests in rural history, family farming, and the environment with my own memories and experiences. I was finding my niche. In the early days of my writing career, though, I didn't think much about what categories my writing fit into. I just knew I wanted to write, and I would prefer to let somebody else worry about how to label or describe my work.

Not long after publishing *The Land Still Lives*, I learned a valuable lesson about publishing, one I never forgot. After seeing some success with my first book, I looked forward to publishing more. During my years working for the University of Wisconsin, I had attended and later run hundreds if not thousands of departmental meetings—so many that I decided to write a book about how to conduct meetings. I assumed that the working world was filled with thousands of meeting leaders who would purchase my book. And this time I wanted a New York publisher. Talking with some writer friends had led me to believe that without a New York publisher, a book would end up selling only a handful of copies and would soon be forgotten. I asked Bob Gard about New York publishers, and he suggested one he had worked with, October House, with offices in Manhattan.

Bob set up a meeting for me with an October House editor, and I made arrangements to fly to New York. My round-trip airfare from Madison to New York cost $128. I had ridden in military planes and helicopters during my

THE
LAND
STILL
LIVES

by Jerry Apps

army stint, but this would be my first trip on a commercial airplane. It also would be my first time in New York City. I was beyond excited.

Bob suggested I make a reservation at the Algonquin Hotel, where, he told me, famous writers gathered. I arrived at LaGuardia Airport, found a taxi, and soon reached the Algonquin. Walking through the lobby, I glanced around to see if I might spot a famous writer. All I saw were ordinary people—but then I realized that I couldn't picture any famous writers other than Ernest Hemingway and F. Scott Fitzgerald.

My meeting at October House was set for the next morning. Before leaving the hotel, I had breakfast with a cup of coffee that cost a dollar—with no refills. (I had never paid more than twenty-five cents for a cup of coffee, including refills, in Madison!) I caught a cab and soon was standing at the reception desk at October House Publishing. I knew things weren't going to go well when the receptionist looked at the editor's schedule and said, "I'm sorry, he seems to have forgotten about your meeting. Could you come back another day?"

Crestfallen, I explained that I had come all the way from Wisconsin and it would be nearly impossible to set up another meeting. "I'll see what I can do," the receptionist said as she picked up the phone.

After a forty-five-minute wait, the editor appeared, and soon I was sitting in his office. I had sent my manuscript in advance, and he had it on his lap. Things were looking up. He looked at me and said, "Jerry, tell me what your book is about."

I began talking about my book, going on at length about what I believed it was about. After a few minutes he interrupted me with these words: "Tell me what your book is about in one or two sentences."

I stammered, "But I just did."

"I'm afraid not," he said sternly. "If you can't tell me what your book is about in a sentence or two, you don't know what it's about. Why don't you go back to Wisconsin and figure out what your book is about and get in touch with me again."

He handed me the manuscript and showed me to the door. The meeting had taken all of fifteen minutes. I felt like a horse had kicked me in the stomach. I stuffed the pages of my manuscript into my briefcase and left. The receptionist didn't even look up when I walked past her desk, and I wondered if she'd seen this happen before, with other wannabe New York authors.

As I flew back to Wisconsin with my hopes of getting a New York publisher dashed, I thought about the editor's comment: "If you can't tell me what your book is about in a sentence or two, you don't know what it's about." Between airfare, cab rides, the hotel bill, and one-dollar coffee, it was an expensive lesson—but one I have remembered ever since. I decided to put my guidebook for better meetings on the shelf for a while. And I began thinking that if I wanted to pursue a career in writing, I would have to learn to think more like the publishing professionals who dealt in genres and marketing plans and "how to describe your book in a sentence or two."

4 Barns of Wisconsin

A couple years after *The Land Still Lives* was published, my secretary at the UW College of Agricultural and Life Sciences told me the dean wanted to speak with me. Expecting the worst—a talk with the dean usually meant I had done something wrong—I left my office on the second floor of Agriculture Hall and headed to Dean Pound's office on the east end of the first floor.

"Jerry, it's good to see you," he said. I was waiting for the second shoe to drop. "I've really enjoyed reading your *Land Still Lives* book," he continued.

Now I was wondering where the discussion was headed.

"Allen Strang and I belong to the same church, and we were talking the other day about his interests and your book."

"You were?" I stammered.

"You probably know that Allen heads up Strang Associates architectural firm here in Madison."

"I didn't know that," I confessed, more confused than ever.

"Anyway, Allen has had a longtime interest in the state's old barns. He has made sketches of many of them and has even done a few watercolor paintings—he's quite a good artist."

I sat with my hands on my lap. So far the discussion was not remotely related to my work as a professor in one of the departments the dean supervised.

"Allen is interested in publishing his barn sketches and paintings, and we were wondering if you might have time to write the captions for his work. It shouldn't take you more than a weekend or two to do it."

"Sure," I said. I'd been teaching college long enough to know that when the dean asked you to do something, you said yes.

"Good," Dean Pound said. "I'll tell him you're willing to do it."

A day or two later I got a phone call from Strang Associates. "Mr. Strang wishes to talk with you," a voice on the other end of the line said. I had done a little checking and learned that not only had Allen Strang started the firm, he was the principal owner.

"Dean Pound and I were talking about your book, *The Land Still Lives*, last Sunday after church," Allen told me, "and he said he'd talked with you about doing some captions for my barn illustrations."

"Yes, we talked," I said.

"I'd like to invite you for lunch at the Black Hawk Country Club. I'll show you some examples of what I've been doing."

"Sure," I said. I knew about the Black Hawk Country Club. It was out of my financial league. When I shared this information with Ruth, all she could say was, "Really?"

A few days later I was sitting across from Allen in the club's dining room. I could see the golf course and, a bit farther away, the waters of Lake Mendota. Allen, in his early seventies and of slight build, told me that he was retiring from his work as an architect and wanted to return to his first love, sketching and painting old barns. He said that during his college years, he had studied watercolor painting, and now, so many years later, he was picking it back up.

He began showing me examples of his work, which I quickly saw was far beyond amateurish. As I looked at the sketches and paintings and we talked, I discovered that although Allen had a great appreciation for old barns, he knew little about them. He showed me a sketch that was meticulously detailed, right down to a metal track that ran from one of the barn doors to the outside. "What's this track for?" he asked.

"That's for the manure carrier," I said. We'd had one like it on the home farm.

He went on showing me sketches and asking me questions. After dessert, he asked, "Could you write captions for me? I've mentioned this project to another friend of mine, Howard Mead, who publishes *Wisconsin Trails* magazine—he is moving into book publishing, and he said he'd meet with me to discuss publishing my barn sketches and paintings. Could you come along with me to the meeting?" He told me the date and time.

I fished out my little pocket calendar, checked the date, and said, "Sure."

A few days later Allen, Howard Mead, and I sat in the Wisconsin Trails conference room with Allen's barn art spread on the table in front of us. After looking through the various sketches and paintings, Howard said, "This is really good work, Allen, but I don't think it would sell as a book. Most people want more than merely pictures."

Allen looked a bit stunned.

Allen Strang and I review his illustrations for the first edition of *Barns of Wisconsin*

Then Howard looked at me. "Would you be up to writing a book on the history of Wisconsin barns that would include Allen's sketches and paintings?" he asked.

"Maybe" was all I could think to say. I had come to the meeting with the idea of spending a couple of weekends writing captions. An entire book would take at least a year to write, I guessed, with six months of research and another six, maybe more, to do the writing and revising. I was teaching full-time at the university, and this work would have to be done on weekends and vacation time. But I knew what I had in my favor was plenty of information about old barns that I had gained from my years growing up on a farm and visiting many of our neighbors' barns during threshing and other community work bees. I accepted the job.

A year later, I had finished writing the book, turned in the manuscript, and responded to some minor editorial questions and comments. Published in 1977, *Barns of Wisconsin* has been reprinted and revised several times since, most recently by the Wisconsin Historical Society Press. It is one of my best-selling books about Wisconsin history—and it hadn't even been my idea to write it.

5 Sources of Ideas

"Where do you get your ideas for writing?" It's the question I'm most frequently asked. Many of my ideas flow from my memories of growing up on a farm. My memory of that time is enhanced by my mother's account books, which she kept during the years she and my father farmed and where she recorded, in pencil, every penny of income and every nickel spent. (That account book led to my book *Every Farm Tells a Story*.) Additional memory joggers for those early years are conversations with my twin brothers, Donald and Darrel, and old photographs of family and neighborhood gatherings.

There was a time when I didn't consider those farm memories to have much value. When I went off to college on a scholarship in 1951, everything about living in the city was unfamiliar to me. I missed country life. But I discovered that most of my fellow students had not grown up in such "primitive" conditions—as one of my new classmates had referred to my life back home. For a time, I felt ashamed of my background, and I vowed to become more like my "sophisticated" fellow students.

It was several years later, while I was on active duty stationed at Fort Eustis, Virginia, that I had an epiphany.

Story ideas often come from my family, friends, neighbors, and old photographs like this one of me with my brothers and our pal Lee Brownlow taken around 1944.

I was thinking about my growing-up years and all that I didn't have—and I began to think of what I *did* have. When I compared my experiences to those of my fellow army officers from New York, Philadelphia, Chicago, and other major cities, I saw that growing up on a farm was special. I came to realize that I had learned much during those years, lessons that had application well beyond the farm: appreciating the land and learning to care for it. Living close to nature, its plants and animals, and the many lessons they subtly taught. Learning the joy of hard work and the feeling of accomplishment that follows a job done well.

Understanding the value of neighbors and the power of community. Helping others who have less. Even though I knew some thought I had been deprived, I decided that instead of being embarrassed and ashamed by what I had experienced, I should be proud of it and share it with others.

Many years later, I heard an interview with a World War II veteran in which he said, "People today, especially those with no direct knowledge of World War II, need to know what war was like and how much each person was expected to contribute. That's why the stories must be told." Later, I wrote this in my journal:

> Writing about my earlier rural life has a similar purpose, to help people with no direct knowledge of early family farm life learn how much the values these farmers held have influenced several generations of our society today. For those who grew up on farms, it was a reminder. For many others it was new information. The challenge is to make my writing compelling, through storytelling and attention to detail.

Along with my memories, my family is a source of writing ideas. Once during lunch with my daughter, as we were talking about possible new topics for my writing, she asked, "Didn't you manage a pickle factory when you were in college?"

"I did—for four summers," I answered.

"Don't you have some stories to tell from that experience?" she asked. After some thinking and several drafts, the result was my novel *In a Pickle*.

For twenty-five years, my son Steve and I canoed in the Boundary Waters of northern Minnesota. We would set up camp and remain there for a week, fishing, relaxing, and enjoying the quiet. In the evenings, we sat by the campfire and looked at the nearby lake, gazed at the night sky, and came up with new writing topics for me. One of the books resulting from those trips is *Campfires and Loon Calls*.

Occasionally, one of my editors suggests an idea for a book. A few years ago, editor Kate Thompson, now the director of the Wisconsin Historical Society Press, asked me if I would be interested in doing a book on farm cooking. I said, "Probably not. The little cooking I do, I never use a recipe."

Then I remembered that I had my mother's old recipe box. Kate suggested the book include stories and menus alongside the recipes—memories of threshing meals, gathering produce from my mother's garden, our Thanksgiving menu, and so on. I talked with Ruth, who in addition to being the first reader of all my work is a professional home economist. She declined to be a coauthor but said she would help with recipe testing if Susan wrote the recipes. The result was *Old Farm Country Cookbook*. It was also Kate who suggested I write about my experience having had polio as a boy in 1947. That conversation led to the publication of *Limping through Life: A Farm Boy's Polio Memoir* in 2013.

There are many obstacles on the path to publication, and of course some ideas never come to fruition. Here is an example, as described in my journal in December 1998:

On Tuesday I met with Mary Braun, editor at the University of Wisconsin Press, to discuss future book projects. I shared with her my idea for a book about the changes agriculture faced during the years 1945–1960. She seemed moderately interested and took some notes. I don't know

My mother's handwritten
recipes, including this one for
bachelor button cookies, inspired
the book *Old Farm Country Cookbook*.

how we got around to deer hunting, but we did. She asked me if I would be interested in writing a book of deer-hunting stories. I was so surprised I didn't know what to say. UW Press was the last publisher in the world that I thought would be interested in a book on deer hunting. I have many deer-hunting and other hunting stories from my growing up years on the farm.

A few days later, I wrote in my journal: "I'm still fussing with the idea for a hunting book for UW Press. I wrote a few stories. I'll try to write a draft proposal this morning, which I will share with Steve, who is my hunting partner these days." After discussing the idea with Steve, I made a few changes and additions to the proposal and sent it off. I had written a couple of chapters and found it to be a more interesting project than I had thought it would be. In my mind I could already see the book in print and selling well.

I waited to hear from the UW Press. Finally, in May 1999, I received an email from Mary Braun. She, along with the press's publicist and direct mail manager, had been laid off. She wrote, "I do urge you to complete *Three Generations of Hunters* when time allows you to do so. No doubt you will find another press eager to publish it. Thanks again for your input on Upper Midwestern topics." The deer-hunting book was never published.

I have never been short on ideas for my writing—they seem to come at me from every direction these days. Ideas are frequently offered to me when I do book presentations and signings. One of the most popular suggestions: "When are you going to write a book about outhouses?"

"Probably never," I answer. I have too many unpleasant memories of outhouses, as our home farm had no indoor plumbing.

Librarians and booksellers have also been a frequent source of ideas for my books. A few years ago, while I was attending the Midwest Booksellers Association fall trade show in Minneapolis, I was catching up with my old friend Jane Janke of Janke Book Store in Wausau. Jane asked, "Have you ever thought of writing a book about the Civilian Conservation Corps? Lots of folks here in the north remember the CCC." The result of that conversation was *The Civilian Conservation Corps in Wisconsin: Nature's Army at Work*, published by the Wisconsin Historical Society Press in 2019.

Booksellers like Jane Janke know what readers are looking for. For me they are a reliable source of topics of interest. *Courtesy of the University of Wisconsin Press*

Occasionally a new writing idea surfaces while I'm working on another project. When I was working on a revision of *Barns of Wisconsin*, I decided to include some unusual barns along with the more traditional ones. I knew about the elephant barn at Circus World Museum in Baraboo, and I drove to Baraboo to meet with then Circus World archivist Fred Dahlinger. He walked me through not only the elephant barn, but the horse barn and camel barn as well. When we finished the tour, Fred said, "Have you thought about writing a book about Circus World Museum? As you know, this was the winter quarters for the Ringling Brothers' Circus for many years."

I dismissed the idea, as I had several other writing projects in the works. In a follow-up visit to Circus World, Fred asked me again about a book on the history of the Ringlings' winter quarters. I said I thought the winter quarters story should be part of a larger book on the Ringlings, and that I wasn't the guy to do it, as I had never even seen a circus as a kid. On a list of topics I knew little about, the circus would be in the top five.

Then Fred said something I hadn't expected. "You are just the kind of person who *should* write the story because you would come at it fresh, without any prejudices." He offered to help me with the research.

I was hooked. I spent untold hours in the archives at Circus World Museum in Baraboo, reading old newspapers and digging into the famous brothers' history. At Fred's suggestion, I traveled to Columbus, Ohio, to meet with a Ringling buff who had purchased several Ringling account books and other records. I spent much of a week there poring over Ringling materials. The result was the book *Ringlingville USA*, published by the Wisconsin Historical Society Press in 2004.

Not every idea becomes a full-length book, of course. When I have identified something I want to write about, I consider what format (article, column, blog post, full book) and what genre (history, memoir, fiction) works best for the topic.

Here is a recent example. For a dozen years or more, the water table at my farm had been dropping. My two ponds, several acres each when they are at their prime levels, were fast becoming mere marshy puddles. They are water table ponds, meaning they have no inlets or outlets; they rise and fall with the water table. Other lakes in the area suffered in a similar fashion. Lake property owners complained—they were paying property taxes befitting a lake home, and now their homes looked out over what looked like a cow pasture. Then, things took a turn. Several years of heavy rainfall recharged the water table until it reached levels not even the oldest of the old-timers remembered. Lakes and ponds ran over; roads flooded; water surrounded farm buildings and changed the landscape.

To consider who might publish a piece on this theme, I turned to the Internet to see what else had been written about it. I found a few related articles, but none that focused on central Wisconsin. Next I asked myself, what should I write? I could easily write a blog entry. At about 250 words plus a photo, they don't take long to write. Or, I could write something slightly longer for one of the two columns I write every month. Should I attempt to write an article of two thousand words or so and submit it to magazines? Or should it be a nonfiction book? That would require at least fifty thousand words—a major commitment of time and energy and many hours of research.

I decided to start with a blog to test the idea. If the reactions were positive, perhaps I would write an article. I wrote the post, published it, and awaited the results. Interest in the blog post was modest. Despite my personal interest, the readership for the topic was not huge. I put further writing on this topic on the back burner.

I am constantly sorting and considering ideas in this way, and many never make it into print. This is especially true for my fiction writing. I have four or five novels in various stages of completion, including one that has been rejected more times than I want to confess.

6 First Fiction

Early in my career, I had developed the misguided idea
that if I wanted to be known as a "real writer," I had to
publish at least one book of poetry and one novel. And
so I sat down and wrote a book of poetry. Ever since
grade school, when I first read poems such as "The Village Blacksmith" by Henry Wadsworth Longfellow and
"The Road Less Traveled" by Robert Frost, I'd had a love
for poetry. I sent my thin manuscript of poems off to a
publisher, fully expecting a quick "We like your poetry
and are pleased to publish it" in response. A few weeks
later, I received a formal note, without even so much as a
handwritten signature, that read, "We are sorry, but your
recent submission does not meet our needs." Even Ruth
quietly said about my attempt at a book of poetry, "It's not
very good." I reached the sad conclusion that my poetry
was several notches below awful and should be relegated
to the back of the rejected-manuscripts file. So much for
my career as a poet.

But my interest in writing fiction persisted. By
the early 1970s, I had written several fictional stories,
some as long as five thousand words. But could I complete a novel, which would have to be a minimum of fifty

thousand words? I had read many novels, of course, and several how-to books on novel writing. I tried to put together my newfound knowledge about the importance of character, sense of place, plot, conflict, suspense, detail, show-don't-tell, and more. It seemed like an impossible task. Looking back on my failure with poetry, I wondered: would my attempt at writing a novel face the same fate? I decided to find out.

John Steinbeck's *The Grapes of Wrath* was the kind of fiction I wanted to write. Maybe that was because I was born in the middle of the Great Depression and knew firsthand the devastation it caused so many people. Perhaps that novel also struck a chord with me because I knew migrant workers who worked in Waushara County cucumber fields when I was growing up and saw their challenging living conditions as they toiled long hours under the torrid summer sun. I was impressed that Steinbeck was not afraid to take on a major issue of the day, the fate of thousands of rural people moving from the lower Midwest to California in search of work and a new life and finding bitter disappointment. I was impressed when I read that Steinbeck had struggled mightily writing *The Grapes of Wrath*. I, too, was struggling to put words on paper, even more than I did when writing nonfiction. When I mentioned this to a friend, he said, "Why don't you stick with what you know how to do? Keep writing nonfiction and let the novelists write the novels."

My friend's comment did not persuade me to stop; in fact, it had the opposite effect. Who says a nonfiction writer couldn't—or shouldn't—write a novel? I thought. But what should I write about? What problem could I tackle following Steinbeck's example in *The Grapes of Wrath*? I thought about the niche I had established for myself in writing about rural life and country living, and I decided to write about a problem many farm kids faced: whether to return to the farm and follow in the footsteps of their parents and grandparents or pursue a dream different from farming.

I could draw on my own experience to explore this theme. When I had decided to attend college rather than taking up farming, it had not been an easy choice. To make my novel more compelling, I would design an even more difficult choice for my main character, the son of a farmer who expected his son to farm after graduating from high school. I placed my novel in a community similar to the one where I grew up and modeled one of my main characters after a slow-talking, elderly professor who had retired in our community made up of farmers. And I wrote the piece in first person, as the main character was somewhat like me—but different from me as well.

I struggled for most of 1982 to write the novel. Finally, I had about forty thousand words, a little short for an adult novel, but perhaps about the right length for a middle-school chapter book. I submitted it to the editor at Stanton & Lee, a small Madison publisher that had expressed interest in my writing. Stanton & Lee agreed to publish it, and within a few weeks I received several pages of notes with suggestions on how to improve the book. For a couple of weeks, I worked on revisions, and then I turned in the manuscript once more. By that time the editor and I had agreed on a title, *The Wild Oak*. I was on my way to having my first novel in print. I was elated.

Soon Stanton & Lee contacted me to ask if I would mind waiting for six months before they published *The Wild Oak*. They were working on publishing the prints of famed wildlife artist Owen Gromme, and it was proving to be a more expensive project than they had anticipated. I agreed. Six months passed, and Stanton & Lee contacted me with unwelcome news: they were canceling the contract for *The Wild Oak*.

I sent the manuscript to a few other publishers, with no success. I was thirty-eight at the time. I knew many successful novelists had published their first novels in their twenties. Should I forget about writing a novel? I immersed myself in writing memoirs and rural history nonfiction books and tried to set aside my aspirations. But the dream never completely died.

7 *Breweries of Wisconsin*

Barns of Wisconsin had marked the beginning of a long collaboration with the editors at Wisconsin Trails. Not long after publishing *Barns*, Trails released *Mills of Wisconsin*, again with illustrations by Allen Strang. A couple of years later, around 1982, Allen and I met with publisher Howard Mead at the Trails office to discuss future book projects.

I believe it was Howard who mentioned that he knew of no book on the history of Wisconsin breweries. Would I have any interest in writing one? he asked. My quick answer was, "I don't think so." True, I enjoyed the occasional glass of beer, but that's about as far as my interest in breweries went. I did know that there had been many local brewers operating near where I grew up, in Berlin (Berliner Beer), Princeton (Tiger Brew), and Stevens Point (Point Special). Allen offered that he might be interested in drawing pictures of the historic breweries that were still standing. I said I'd have to think about it. I knew I would be starting from scratch with the research. I knew a lot about barns, having essentially grown up in one. But I had no experience with breweries. I had never been inside one.

After a couple of days of considering and discussing the matter with Ruth, I called Howard and said I would do it, but that I would need a couple thousand dollars in advance to cover my travel expenses. To research the book, I knew I would have to do considerable traveling around the state. When the advance check arrived, I began a two-year adventure visiting breweries and talking with retired and working brewmasters. My son Steve was getting started in his career as a professional photographer, and he traveled with me, enjoying the free beer we received at each brewery we visited.

In addition to visiting breweries and interviewing people involved in the business, I dug out old newspaper stories about breweries and looked at early advertisements. Soon I had ample material, and by 1984 I had a draft manuscript ready for the Wisconsin Trails staff to read.

But then the unexpected happened. Howard Mead called to say that the company's book editor had left for another job, and Trails probably wouldn't be replacing him. "We will not be able to publish your brewery book," he told me.

"What about the advance money you sent me?" I asked.

"You can keep it."

With the advance mostly spent and with seventy-five thousand words or so of manuscript written and a number of illustrations completed, Allen and I found ourselves without a publisher. I contacted Stanton & Lee, who had recently accepted my short novel *The Wild Oak*. They said they'd have their editor look over the manuscript and illustrations and get back to me. I said I would need an advance in the same amount I had gotten from Trails.

A few weeks later came the response: "Our editor has some suggested changes and additions, but this looks like something we can do." In a few days the advance check arrived. I breathed a sigh of relief. I had had visions of the draft manuscript sitting on my shelf next to other failed publishing projects.

The revisions the editor asked for were extensive and took me several months to complete. One of the problems I faced was that the brewing industry was in turmoil. Brewing in the 1980s was undergoing consolidation, and closings were happening all around the state. It was difficult to keep up with the latest developments.

In 1986 or 1987, I turned in the revised manuscript. I waited patiently for further comments from the Stanton & Lee editor. Finally, I heard more disappointing news: The company was in financial trouble. Not only was *The Wild Oak* cancelled, but *Breweries* was out, too.

"What about the advance you paid me?" I asked.

"You can keep it," I heard back.

Once again, the revised Wisconsin brewery history landed on my shelf of unpublished projects. On the plus side, with the two advances, I had earned about as much money as I had received for some of my earlier published books—although by this time I had spent much of it on travel and other research expenses.

I let the project rest and turned to other writing. But eventually I wondered, after spending so much time and effort researching and writing the book, was I being fair to myself by giving up? I had heard that writer George Vukelich and his friend Jerry Minnich had opened a small publishing house. I met with them for lunch one day in about 1989 and showed them the Wisconsin brewery history project.

They seemed interested, but they quickly said that their new company did not have the resources to publish what would be a sizable book with many illustrations. Before I could express my disappointment in now having three publishers say no to my project, Jerry said, "I have an idea for you."

"I'm listening," I said, expecting him to suggest further revisions and changes to the manuscript.

"I used to work for the University of Wisconsin Press," he said. "They might be interested in this book. They are starting a new series focusing on Wisconsin topics."

This idea stopped me completely. This was well before my encounter with Mary Braun and the deer-hunting book, and I believed the UW Press's publishing was mostly associated with UW professors' research findings. I had never thought of them as a publisher for my books.

Following Jerry's advice, I shared the brewery manuscript and illustrations with Mary. I heard back quickly that, yes, they were interested in publishing the book—but without Allen Strang's illustrations. Allen was a bit surprised at their dismissal of his work, but he didn't seem too disturbed when he learned the reason. They wanted to use historic photos from the Wisconsin Historical Society photo archives collection and even volunteered to have one of their staff members research and obtain the WHS photos.

After more revision, *Breweries of Wisconsin* was finally published in 1992, ten years after I began working on it. The book quickly sold more than five thousand copies. By the early 2000s, the brewing industry was growing rapidly again, with small craft breweries pop-

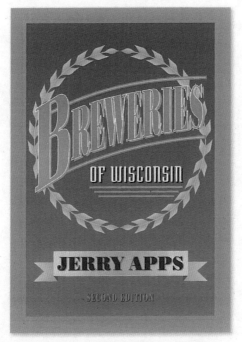

Courtesy of the University of Wisconsin Press

ping up around the state, and I wrote a revised edition of the book for the UW Press in 2005. *Breweries of Wisconsin* remains in print and, with more than twelve thousand copies sold, is an example of one of my most successful books.

8 Full-time Writer

In the fall of 1992, I was busy doing promotional appearances for *Breweries of Wisconsin*. After my presentations, I always chatted with people while signing the copies they had purchased. At a bookstore in Waupaca, not far from where I grew up, one of the last people in line was a woman who introduced herself as Roberta Spanbauer, the editor at Amherst Press, based in Amherst, Wisconsin. She said that she and her husband, Chuck Spanbauer, had taken over what had been Palmer Publications and had published several cookbooks, including some related to Wisconsin bed-and-breakfasts. Amherst Press was interested in expanding its operations, she told me, and asked if I had any interest in writing a book for them.

I didn't give her invitation much thought. I was still teaching full-time, and I was writing an academic book. I said, "Send me something," and gave her my mailing address. In a few days, a couple of Amherst cookbooks arrived in the mail, along with a letter inviting me to send a book proposal. This was the first time I had received such an invitation, and I was flattered. I'd spent many hours seeking publishers for my books. This seemed too easy.

I had long been interested in writing a book about one-room country schools. I had many stories from the eight years I attended the one-room Chain O' Lake School, and I knew Ruth had stories from her one-room school experience as well. With her help, I wrote a proposal and sent it off to Amherst Press.

A week or so later I received a reply. The Spanbauers were interested in the project, but they were worried that the market for such a book would be slim. They asked if I would drive up to Amherst and meet with them.

Arriving in Amherst, I discovered that the press was located in a former school building, with the offices and editorial staff on the second floor, a printing shop on the first floor, and the distribution center in the basement. We met for an hour or so and talked mostly about the idea's market potential. I said that although one-room schools had closed in the 1960s, a good number of former students, as well as their teachers, were still alive and well and, I believed, would be interested in such a book. Thinking Amherst wouldn't be interested in publishing a memoir, I didn't share with them that one of the reasons I wanted to write the book was to relive my eight years attending the Chain O' Lake School, District Number 4, in the Township of Rose. I explained more about what I had in mind for the book and how I planned doing the research, which included collecting stories from former students and teachers as well as my and Ruth's stories.

Rather reluctantly, they agreed to publish the book, and they released *One-Room Country Schools* in 1996. Amherst went all out with a marketing plan, sending promotional information to all the bookstores and gift shops in the state that had been carrying their cookbooks. They sent order forms to members of the Wisconsin Retired

Teachers Association offering a 5 percent discount on purchases of the book and arranged for me to speak at the association's annual meeting in Stevens Point.

During my presentation, I talked about the poetry we had memorized in grade school, and I recited a bit from "The Village Blacksmith" by Henry Wadsworth Long-fellow: "Under a spreading chestnut-tree, / The village smithy stands; / The smith, a mighty man is he . . ." The entire audience began reciting the poem with me. It was a poignant moment that I've never forgotten.

The audience had made a connection to the book because they had a similar experience to what I had de-scribed. And I had learned an important lesson. When people feel a connection to something, they become en-gaged. Since that time, I have worked hard to help people feel a personal connection to my books, presentations, and TV shows.

Ruth sold about twenty books that day. Interest in the topic was much greater than I imagined it would be. Not long after the book came out, I appeared on a Wisconsin Public Radio show with host Larry Meiller. At the end of the forty-five-minute show, I provided Amherst Press's phone number and said that anyone interested in pur-chasing a copy of the book should call them. The next day, my editor at Amherst said, "We got phone calls all afternoon, and we even had to have someone answering the phone after closing time. Never saw so much interest in a book." Sales far exceeded what Amherst Press had expected.

By the time *One-Room Country Schools* was released in 1996, I had committed to writing full-time and left my position at the University of Wisconsin. Before consid-ering new writing projects, I had to complete a few that I had started during my final teaching days. One was a revision of *Barns of Wisconsin*, which by 1995 had sold sixteen thousand copies and which Wisconsin Trails had asked me to bring up to date with a revised edition to assure continued sales. But by midyear, I was contemplating another book idea: I wanted to collect the country sayings of my father, our neighbors, and other rural people I had known, including those I had worked with during my years as a county extension agent. I called this material "rural wisdom": "No dew on the morning grass, rain before noon," "Never go outside without wearing your shirt; if God had meant for you to run around naked, you would have been born that way," "No matter what direction a North Wind blows in winter, it always blows cold," "If you are doing nothing, how do you know when you are finished?"

By this time I had enlisted the help of a literary agent. Upon reviewing my chapter outline and sample text, she said, "I'm sorry, Jerry, but I don't think any publisher will want to publish this book. And to be frank with you, I doubt more than a handful of readers would read it, either."

Ignoring her comments, I contacted Amherst Press, half expecting them to turn it down. *Rural Wisdom* was considerably different from anything they had published. After I discussed the book proposal with the Stanbauers, they said they'd get back to me. Later I learned that they struggled over the decision just as they had with *One-Room Country Schools*. In the end, they published *Rural Wisdom*, which came out in 1997. It immediately sold well and went on to be one of my best-selling nonfiction books.

Earlier in the year, I had learned the surprising news that I was the 1996 winner of the Robert E. Gard Award for

Excellence, given by the Robert E. Gard Foundation and the Wisconsin Academy of Sciences, Arts, and Letters to honor an individual's "commitment to fostering healthy communities through arts-based development." The award included a five-hundred-dollar honorarium and a certificate. Previous winners included children's book writer Kevin Henkes, poets Ron Wallace and Roberta J. Hill, and playwright David Peterson. As my first year of full-time writing was coming to an end, I had begun to see some real success in my publishing endeavors. But I wondered if the books I was working on, especially *Rural Wisdom*, would sell as well as the barn and brewery books. I always tried to follow my father's advice: "Do the best you can with what you've got." But was my best good enough? No matter how many books I write or how many years I spend doing it, it's a question I still ask myself.

9   Essentials for Writing

By the time I committed to full-time writing in 1996, I had
several books under my belt and had learned a lot about
what writing techniques and habits work well for me. For
example, my most productive and creative writing time is
in the morning. My creative juices begin to dry up by early
afternoon, and by evening they all but disappear. When I
was teaching full-time, I got up at 5:30 every day, while the
rest of the family was sleeping, and wrote for a couple of
hours before I traveled to the campus.

For many years I have taken a walk, at least a half
mile, before I eat breakfast and sit down at my computer
to work. During my morning walk, I think about what
I'm going to write that day. In a way, I am outlining my
day's work as I am exercising. I try to be at my writing
desk by 8:00 every morning, six days a week. I do little
or no writing on Sunday—unless a really important idea
pops into my head and I fear I will forget the nuances
of it unless I write it down. On my writing days, I write
for a couple of hours, take a brief break, and write until
noon. I try to write a thousand words a day. Some days I
do more, some days less. After lunch and a nap (I never
want to miss a nap), I answer emails or do research.

My writing students often ask where I write. During my teaching years, when I traveled a good deal, I learned to write in airport terminals, restaurants, and hotel rooms. These weren't ideal writing places, but it was either write there or not at all. At home, I wrote in my basement "office." Ruth and I had agreed I could hire a carpenter to make the windowless room a bit more inviting as soon as my writing brought in enough money to pay for it. Eventually my writing income picked up enough so that, in 1998, I met with an architect to plan a thirteen-by-fourteen-foot office addition to our home. It would have a door to an outside patio and windows that looked out on the backyard. Now I would have room for bookshelves, filing cabinets, a big storage cabinet, and a spacious computer desk with room for files and a printer. We did other remodeling of the house as well—and took on a second mortgage. It was a major improvement from my rather dusty, dismal writing quarters in a back corner of our basement. And I discovered what so many others have, that having a dedicated place for writing is essential. As one of my writing students said, "I write on the kitchen table. But this means I have to clear it before I can begin writing. By the time I finish clearing the table and finding my laptop and other writing supplies, my creativity has gone out the window."

Some of my writing friends write in coffee shops—for them, there is something about the ambience that enhances their creativity. But it doesn't work for me. I write best in a place that is quiet, without interruption.

I also write in a dedicated room in the cabin at my farm. Although there is no internet connection, the place is quiet, and the rural views out the window are never tiring—although they are occasionally interrupted, as they

A dedicated writing spot has been essential for me. I have now written part of at least thirty books at this desk in my Madison home office.

were in May one year when out of the corner of my eye I saw two fawns, still with spots, playing not more than twenty-five yards from where I was writing. On occasion I might see a wild turkey prancing outside my window. There's always a variety of birds. I see these not as disruptions but as enhancements to my writing.

When it comes to the tools of writing, at the most basic level, all I need is paper and pen. But while I do plenty of writing in longhand, I learned early on that if I wanted my material to be published, it had to be typed. I was fortunate that I had followed that teacher's advice in high school and taken a typing course. I was so taken with typing that by the end of the first semester, I bought my own typewriter, a Remington portable, which I have to this day (though I haven't used it in years). I used my Remington for typing my high school papers, I used it all through my college years, and I typed my first book on it.

Along the way I learned to think about what I was going to write and then type it, instead of writing everything out first in longhand and then typing from the written page.

By the 1970s, electric typewriters were available, and although I bought one, I never liked it. I discovered that I had some bad typing habits, one of which was resting my fingers on the keyboard while I was thinking of the next thing to type. Suddenly, strange letters appeared on the page in front of me. It took me several weeks to learn that a soft touch was in order. I also disliked the annoying hum that never quit until I turned off the machine. I like things quiet when I am writing.

The next step in the evolution of my writing tools was an electronic typewriter that I bought in the late 1970s. It displayed several lines of electronic words in a window so I could check for misspellings and correct them before the machine printed the words on paper. The machine was big and clunky. I never liked it. It also had an infernal hum that I detested.

By the early 1980s, the talk was about computers designed for writing, described as word processors. The secretaries in my university office began using Wang computers, but I found those too large and cumbersome. I wanted something that I could carry around, as I was doing my writing both at home and at my farm. The two computers I looked at were an Osborne model, which had a little five-inch built-in monitor, and a Kaypro, which had a nine-inch monitor and came in a steel case. It was advertised as a portable computer, weighing only twenty-eight pounds. I bought one.

My Kaypro was a vast improvement over the electronic typewriter. Its keyboard required a firm touch, and what I wrote was saved electronically on a 5¼-inch floppy disk. The computer program was on a second floppy disk. Best of all: no hum.

By the mid-1980s, computers had left behind the large floppy disks for $3\frac{1}{2}$-inch hard disks. Around 1990, I replaced my trusty Kaypro with a Toshiba laptop, a sturdy, dependable, and much lighter machine. By the late 1990s, I was also using a Dell desktop computer. For more than fifteen years, I wrote on Toshiba laptops, trading for more up-to-date ones about every three to four years. I left Toshibas behind in 2015 and purchased a MacBook Air laptop. Today, I use a MacBook Air along with a Dell desktop computer, a Samsung nineteen-inch monitor, and a Brother compact laser printer.

Despite all this discussion of typewriters and computers, I do not have a love affair with technology. As a writer I see these as necessary tools for doing the work. Pen and pencil continue to serve me well as writing instruments.

Equally essential to my writing are my journals. I kept my first diary during my long recovery from polio at age twelve, and I picked up the practice again as an adult at the suggestion of Al Nelson, who taught the first writing workshop I attended. I have written regularly in a journal ever since. I am currently writing in journal volume 47, which means I have forty-six journals stacked up in my closet.

I write longhand in a hardcover journal. Some have lined pages, and some do not. I discovered long ago that something important happens when I write with pen and paper compared to writing on a keyboard. Sometimes something mysterious, perhaps even magical, occurs when I am writing in longhand. It's as if there is a connection from my brain that runs down my arm to my hand and flows from my pen to the paper. Sometimes

Oct 7 = Sunday
Oct 6 = Sat.

Oct 8, 1979

Yesterday was a fantastic fall day. Steve, two of his friends, and I went up to the farm on Saturday night.

Yesterday morning the ground and the roofs were covered with white frost.

The boys were hunting. I spent the day cutting and splitting wood, and harvesting Indian and pop corn. I also loaded into the car all of the squash and pumpkins we grew this year. It was not a good squash year compared to other years. I would guess there was too much rain during the fruit setting time.

Next Saturday morning Jeff and I will sell at the farmer's market, then go up to the farm in the afternoon for another load of Indian and pop corn.

I constantly marvel at how quiet it is at the farm. Here

A journal entry from October 1979 describes autumn at our farm.

when I am writing in longhand in my journal, I discover I am writing something I had never thought to write, something new and special, something that seems to come from a source I am not aware of.

Writing in longhand slows me down; I can type many times faster on a keyboard. Slowing down allows my brain to catch up with what I am writing. Also, I've discovered that when I face a problem or roadblock in my writing—when I can't find the right words to say or how I want to say them—writing in my journal helps. More times than not, by writing about the problem in my journal, I figure out the answer.

Journaling provides other benefits for me as a writer. My journal is a historical record of my life, the events and people I've encountered and the places I've been. Often these details help with future research and writing projects. For instance, my book *Roshara Journal* includes the story of my farm through journal entries spanning fifty years. Likewise, *Campfires and Loon Calls* draws heavily on journal entries I made during the twenty-five years that my son Steve and I canoed in the Boundary Waters of northern Minnesota.

In my journal I also record the joys and challenges associated with writing. For example, I wrote the following in June 2005:

> Somewhere I read, "It doesn't matter how many times you fall down, but how many times you get up." I'm feeling like one of those down times again. Writing is like that. I've been writing full-time since 1996, and still no book has broken free and hit more than modest sales. . . . Maybe I should just say, "I quit" one of these

days and stop being frustrated. But then what would I do? Time to get up, dust myself off and get back to work.

Looking back at my journal entries keeps me humble about my writing. I know I can do better, and I always strive to do so. There are days when nothing seems to work, the words don't come, the ideas dry up. But I continue on, always looking ahead, always with hope that the writing will be easier and my reader numbers will continue increasing.

In addition to my general journal, I keep a journal for every book I am writing. (This means I have some journals for books that were never published.) For example, for the book *Once a Professor*, I began a book journal on June 5, 2014, with these words: "Is there a book related to my thirty years as a college professor?" I was uncertain about writing the book or what form it should take. "How should I write the book? As a memoir? As a novel? Focus on my entire career? I have lots of information about the inner workings of UW–Madison. Tenure and how to achieve it? What it's like being a department chair? Focus only on the protest years of the late 1960s and early 1970s?" I eventually decided to write the book as a memoir.

In these book journals, I make notes about things I must remember to include and things to leave out, names of people I may want to interview, topics I might need to research, and more. As a motivational tool, I note my writing progress by including the starting word count and ending word count for each day.

For the past twenty-five years, I have also kept a third kind of journal, what I refer to as my "Idea Notebook." It is a 7½-by-5½-inch six-ring leather-covered notebook that I have with me most of the time. I can easily remove the lined pages for filing. When I am waiting at the doctor's or dentist's office, I often jot down ideas. I may make a list of what I believe the components of a book might be. For example, on July 1, 2019, I wrote the following in my idea book:

> The pastor yesterday spoke about the need for, and how people of different backgrounds and different political perspectives can find common ground through joint activities. I am reminded of what my father often said about one of our neighbors who were considerably different from us—they didn't go to church, they cursed a lot, they had an ethnic background different from us. My father said, "They are neighbors and we will work with them." And we did.
>
> Few people live on farms anymore. There is no such thing as a threshing or a wood sawing bee that brought country people together as they helped each other. How can we find common ground with the "other" as people different from us are often called? Where do we start? Does it take a catastrophe to bring people together? A tornado? A fire? A flood?

Those comments by our pastor got me thinking about thinking—critical and creative thinking. I wrote several pages of notes about thinking and the importance of people thinking for themselves rather than depending on other people to think for them. In 2021, I signed a contract with Fulcrum Press for a book on the topic of independent thinking.

My three types of journals are especially helpful when I'm working on several writing projects at the same time.

Here is an example of my projects as I write this: I have two new books coming out this fall. In a few weeks I will be helping with the marketing of those books. I have a new book coming out next spring; I've just finished responding to the copyeditor's comments. Last month I completed the first draft of a manuscript for a major agricultural history book that is due to the publisher this fall. Right now it's resting; I will come back to it next month, when, in addition to revising and rewriting, I will decide on illustration placement.

And, of course I am writing the book you are reading. How do I keep straight in my mind where I am with each project? Writing in my journal and keeping a separate book journal for each project helps me keep all the details in order. Even though I appear to be working on several projects at the same time, I can focus on them one at a time, giving that particular project my full attention.

WRITING PROJECTS: JULY 1, 2014

Here is a snapshot of what I was doing in 2014. Not all of my years were as busy as this one, thankfully.

1. *Whispers and Shadows*. Completed response to final round of editing. Book now in production. Wisconsin Historical Society Press.

2. *The Great Sand Fracas of Ames County*. My fourth novel. Met with marketing people from University of Wisconsin Press, the publisher. Due out in September of this year.

3. *Roshara Journal*. Working on research and writing for this book. Wisconsin Historical Society Press. Steve will do photographs. Manuscript due December 1 of this year.

4. *Telling Your Story*. Fulcrum Press. Manuscript for book due December 1 of this year.

5. *Wisconsin Agriculture: A History*. Wisconsin Historical Society Press. In the editing process of this book. Due out fall of 2015.

6. *Old Farm Country Cookbook.* (With daughter Sue.) Wisconsin Historical Society Press. Manuscript due September 2015. Have 13,000 words in draft.

7. *Once a Professor*. In the idea stage. Will submit a proposal to Wisconsin Historical Society Press.

10 Voice and Approach

With each new writing project I tackled, I was developing my voice as a writer. Voice means putting "me" into my writing. My voice is *how* I say things, which can be as important as *what* I say. It includes my writing style, the words I choose and the way I string them together into sentences and build paragraphs. My voice is also a reflection of my personal history and my perspective on the world. Writing with a particular voice, however, doesn't mean preaching or trying to convince people that what you believe about something is what they should believe.

When I began writing for publication, I decided I wanted my parents to be able to read and understand whatever I wrote. My dad had been pulled out of school after fifth grade to work on the farm; my mother completed seventh grade before she had to drop formal schooling for work. Their lack of formal education didn't mean they weren't interested in reading. They read daily and weekly newspapers and various farm-related magazines. But flowery language did not impress them. They avoided reading what they called "highfalutin'" writing littered with "fifty-cent" words and sentences that seemed to never end.

Before I began writing for general readers, I had spent several years writing and editing academic material, mostly for other academics. During my university years, I worked as a publication editor, an editor of a national professional journal, a book review editor for a professional journal, and a part-time acquisitions/consulting editor for the College Division of the McGraw-Hill Book Company in New York. My writing wasn't simple then. Fifty-cent words were common, and jargon words were not only acceptable but often required. Most of that writing was reviewed by third-party reviewers—other academics who expected an academic writing style that they were accustomed to reading.

But even in my academic writing, as in my teaching, I understood that telling a story was a way to help me reach my audience. Stories entertain, inform, trigger emotions, bring back memories, and cause people to think about things they haven't thought about for a long time, perhaps ever. It seemed natural to incorporate storytelling into my professional writing.

A story is more than words. It can take people to places they have never been. A story can bring people to life, even if they have long been dead or never existed. A story can evoke feelings in people they have thought long forgotten, bringing tears and laughter, sometimes in the same paragraph. Stories are what make us human. Our own stories make us different from one another yet tie us all together. People have stories, but so do buildings, cities, villages, farms, and even trees and prairies, rivers and lakes, and the land. As a writer, I am charged with the task of digging out the stories, some hidden deeply, some just below the surface.

To make my writing easily understandable, I often write short sentences, short paragraphs, and even short chapters when I am writing a book. One editor said to me, after reading a draft of a chapter I was working on, "Have you tried longer sentences?" I wasn't discouraged by her comment, because I understood that she meant that *only* short sentences, without variety, makes for choppy writing and can be boring for the reader. The answer is to write some sentences long, some short, some even shorter. I call this creating a rhythm in writing. Once when I was teaching a writing course at The Clearing in Door County, one of the students was an orchestra director. After a brief discussion of rhythm in writing, he said, "Sounds to me like a good piece of writing is like a good piece of music. There are slow places, faster places, louder places, and quiet places. Places that tap emotions, places that create contemplation." I was pleased to hear my lesson summed up so succinctly.

 I keep my writing style simple. Keeping in mind another of my father's sayings, "Don't brag—nobody likes a bragger," I try to write in a way that draws attention to what I have to say, not how I say it. I would rather have someone comment on an idea I proposed, a story I told, a character I described than tell me how wonderful my writing style was. I put flowery, multisyllable, exceedingly long, adjective-heavy sentences in the category of bragging: "Look at me! See my special way of writing." I relate my dad's saying to what William Strunk and E. B. White said in their famous little writing guide, *The Elements of Style*: "Place yourself in the background." The last thing I want to hear from a reader is, "He has a wonderful way of saying nothing."

I've also found writing about simple things to be an effective approach and have made such topics part of my voice as a writer. In many of my books, I write about the simple yet important objects I recall from growing up on the farm. For example, I wrote this about our barn lantern:

Those of my generation, especially those who grew up on farms before electricity arrived, remember barn lanterns. We all had them, lamps in the house and lanterns outdoors.

On a cold winter morning, after dressing in front of the dining room wood burner, I would pull on my old Mackinaw winter coat, slip on my wool cap with the fur ear laps, and find my barn lantern standing at its place near the wood box in the kitchen. I would take a match from the match box on the wall near the kitchen stove, lift the lantern's glass globe, strike the match, touch the flame to the lantern's wick, and close down the globe. Then I was on my way to the barn, where Pa had gone a few minutes earlier.

The lantern cast long shadows on the snow scape, as I briskly walked along the narrow path we had shoveled in the snow. Once arriving at the barn, I hung my lantern on the nail behind the cows. Pa had hung his lantern on a nail at the other end of the barn. Grabbing up my three-legged milk stool and a milk pail, I cozied up under a cow and began milking. Except for the sound of fresh milk zinging against the bottom of the milk pail and the occasional rattle of a cow's stanchion, it was quiet in the barn. The two lanterns offered just enough light so we could see what we were doing. The soft, yellow light cast by the lanterns added to this quiet, peaceful time.

This may sound weird to some readers, but I have come to believe that every book has its own way of wanting to be written. With many of the books I've written, I have had to write several chapters before I discover how it wants to be written. I struggle with these first chapters. The words and the sentences come painfully slowly. I rearrange the order, consider what themes to develop more fully, and wrestle with what to include and what to leave out. But I plow on, thinking back to previous books that I have written and recalling that I experienced the same thing then, too.

Another important part of developing my voice has been learning to balance my creative self and my judging self. For me as a writer, the creative self is the part of me that is constantly seeking new ideas and new ways of expressing them, trying things that I have not tried before. The judging self is in charge of the rules: spelling rules, grammar rules, rules of logic, and so on. For most of us, our judging self is more developed than our creative self; to put it a bit too simply, we are better at tearing things down than building things up. Through formal schooling, many of us learned how to be critical; it is more difficult to learn creativity. Nonetheless, each of us has a creative self, wanting to express itself and too often prevented from doing so by the ever-present judge.

As a writer, I need both my creative self and my judging self to be well developed. I've also learned how to keep the judging self at bay, for the most part, while the creative self is working. Here is the sort of discussion that often goes on in my head after I write a paragraph: The creative self says to its nemesis, the judging self, "This is really quite a good paragraph, isn't it?" The judging self sniffs, "Good paragraph? It's awful—it's too long, you've misspelled a word, and you've got the commas in the wrong place."

The way I handle this is to keep on writing, allowing the creative self to keep working, and keeping the judging self quiet, not giving it a chance to examine what I've just written. This is why I write a piece—whether it's a 250-word blog or an 80,000-word novel—all the way through and do little editing along the way. The judging self will have its day.

Another technique I have used to keep the judging self from interfering is timed writing. I set a timer for fifteen minutes, and I write until the timer rings. The judge doesn't have a chance to raise its ugly voice and break the momentum of my work.

11 A Low Point

After the success of *One-Room Country Schools* in 1996 and *Rural Wisdom* in 1997, I suggested to Amherst Press a book on the history of cheese making. They published *Cheese: The Making of a Wisconsin Tradition* in 1998. By that fall, *One-Room Country Schools* had sold more than seven thousand copies, and to the surprise of all, *Rural Wisdom* had sold nearly ten thousand copies. I wrote in my journal, "This is by far the best I've ever done with my writing. In one month, *Rural Wisdom* sold nearly 2,000 copies." I met with the owners that September to discuss future book projects.

Amherst published *When Chores Were Done*, stories of my growing-up years on the farm, in 1999, followed by *Symbols: Viewing a Rural Past* later that year. I clearly was on a roll. Ruth and I traveled the state giving talks and selling books. What could be better? And then everything began to unravel.

I wrote the following in my journal on June 25, 2000:

Bad news! I talked with the Amherst people on Friday and their bank has closed them down. When I got back to Madison from my farm, I saw this letter; "It is

Amherst Press created this cutout of a much younger version of me in bib overalls to promote *When Chores Were Done*.

with regret that I must inform you that Amherst Press
(Palmer Publications) has ceased its business operations." The hope is that the Amherst principals can sell
the book division in total. Where does this leave me?
Sad, angry, confused, surprised. I surely didn't see this
coming. The Recession of 2000 has taken its toll.

By late July 2000, Amherst had found a buyer for its
books division. I had signed an agreement allowing my
books and their rights to be part of the purchase. The new
buyer was a small, newly organized publisher located in
northern Wisconsin.

By February 2002, I had the first inkling that my new
publisher was also having financial problems. A partial
royalty check arrived late. But on May 13, 2003, my new
publisher informed me that they had sold several thousand copies of *Rural Wisdom* to the Cracker Barrel restau-
rant chain. That seemed like good news. By early June,
they were doing an eighth printing of *Rural Wisdom*. I
breathed a sigh of relief. My hopes were further buoyed
when I received another partial royalty check on June 23,
2003.

In 2004, royalty payments ceased coming. I had to
make a decision. My attorney said I could sue the publisher because my book contracts were clear about when
royalty payments must be sent, and they had now missed
the last two payments, with no offering of even partial
payments. But suing them for what they owed me would
do little good, as they obviously had no money. I suggested that in lieu of royalty payments, I would take ownership of my book inventory, along with all the rights to
my books that they had acquired. My attorney drew up
a document, the publisher signed it, and I became the

owner of about fourteen thousand copies of my books. But what was I to do with them?

Voyageur Press in Stillwater, Minnesota, had published two of my farm-related books in 2005, and they agreed to buy *Rural Wisdom*, *When Chores Were Done*, *Humor from the Country*, and *Symbols*. Voyageur's purchase price was what the original publisher had paid to have the books printed. With the purchase Voyageur also gained all future printing rights.

I made deals for the other titles as well. The University of Wisconsin Press agreed to distribute *One-Room Country Schools* and *Cheese: The Making of a Wisconsin Tradition*. Partners, a book distributor in Michigan, agreed to distribute two children's picture books I had published with Amherst, *Eat Rutabagas* and *Stormy*.

Before this I knew absolutely nothing about how books were warehoused. I soon learned more than I wanted to know, as Steve and I drove on a cold winter day to the publisher's unheated warehouse in northern Wisconsin to put new labels on the boxes indicating the new owners or distributors. Once the labels were in place, we piled the cartons on pallets and shrink-wrapped them for shipment. Each of the sixty-three cartons of *When Chores Were Done* weighed thirty-one pounds—nearly a ton of books. *Humor from the Country* comprised forty-six cartons at forty-four pounds each, and so on. All together we loaded five pallets of books weighing four and a half tons. I was talking about books in pounds rather than units sold! Freight truckers want to know about pounds.

The episode marked the lowest time in my more than fifty-year writing career. From the beginning, I had wanted to support regional publishers and had enjoyed working with them, discussing potential book projects from the idea to seeing the finished book on a book-seller's shelf. But publishing is a business, and financial concerns must be addressed. Publishers and booksellers are often hit especially hard during recessions, when unemployment rates and the cost of goods soar. When people are concerned about eating and keeping a roof over their heads, they are unlikely to buy a book.

If I had had a literary agent at the time, he or she would have worked all of this out for me—and perhaps would have helped me avoid the situation in the first place. But after dabbling with agents and being turned down by several over the years, most often because they said my work was too regional and would not have national appeal, I had decided to go it alone.

If I could do it all over again, I would not allow the rights and the inventory of my Amherst books to go along with the company's sale to a new publisher. But the part of me that wanted to support and encourage small, regional publishers had overruled my better judgment. I should have asked more questions and done more research about the new publisher. One of my most successful publishing relationships had ended with one of the most disappointing and costly experiences in my long writing career.

12 Writing Memoirs

After my failed attempt to publish my first novel, *The Wild Oak*, in the early 1980s, I had set aside my interest in fiction writing and focused all my attention on writing nonfiction books. When I began to understand how publishers like to categorize things, I wondered, why the title *nonfiction*? Why not say what the writing *is* rather than what it is *not*? To me it was like calling a sunny day a non-cloudy day. So, I did a little digging and discovered this: apparently the naming of certain nonfiction writing material came about in 1867, when a Boston librarian began calling works that were neither poetry nor fiction "not fiction," or more popularly, nonfiction.

Nonfiction is a broad category that encompasses both my history books and my memoir writing. When I began writing memoirs, I didn't know I was doing it. I didn't know the difference between an autobiography and a memoir, a life story or a reminiscence. I learned that a generally accepted definition of *autobiography* is a work in which a person writes about his or her entire life, from birth to the present time. Memoirs, on the other hand, are usually about a particular event or period in a person's life. Both autobiography and memoir are written in the first person.

Where does nostalgia fit in? Nostalgia is sometimes described as a sentimental longing for an earlier day when most everything was better than it is today. Someone once said to me, after I described something I was writing, "Oh, you're writing nostalgia. You'll never get anywhere doing that. Writing critics and reviewers look down their noses at any writing that smells like nostalgia." But in truth, I don't much care if certain people see my writing as nostalgia. I believe my stories of growing up on a farm during the Great Depression and World War II go far deeper than nostalgia, as I examine the stories' meaning to me today and share what I learned from the experience. I try to share not only the wonderful experiences I've had, but also the difficult, frightening, and often sad experiences—the good and the bad all mixed together, and all in a story format. If the stories I write about those times provide a warm feeling for folks who have had similar experiences, frankly, I'm pleased.

Before I begin writing a memoir, I usually create a mind map to help me get in touch with my memories. A mind map is a way of examining an idea from the inside out. I begin by drawing a circle on a sheet of paper and then writing in the circle the idea I want to examine. For instance, if I want to discover my memories about an event I experienced, such as my first day attending a one-room school, I write, "First day at a one-room school." Then I draw lines and circles extending from the big circle where I write all the good and bad memories of my first day of school. After I've completed the initial mind map, I ask myself a question: What are the stories connected to each of these memories? For example, for my book *The Quiet Season*, about winters on the farm, I wrote down a memory of a morning when it was twenty below zero. So what? How did a bitterly cold morning affect me and my family? Reflecting on what stories are associated with the memory led to these paragraphs from the chapter titled "Below-Zero Morning":

> I was awakened by the *tap, tap* of Pa gently rapping the stove poker on the stovepipe below our bedroom floor. It was my wakeup call, Pa's way of telling me it was six o'clock and time to roll out of bed, dress, and hurry out to the barn for the morning milking. I wouldn't know until I glanced at the outside porch thermometer on my way to the barn that it was twenty degrees below zero.
>
> The fire in the dining room stove usually went out around midnight, and now the upstairs bedroom was nearly as cold as outside. I stuck a wool sock–covered foot out of my warm bed and thumped it a couple of times on the floor, hoping Pa would think I was up and dressing. But he had long known my ploy and tapped once more on the stovepipe, a little louder this time, letting me know there was work to do.

The process continues as I consider each memory and think about the stories connected to it. Of course, as I write, more memories surface. I write my stories as truthfully as I can, as I remember them. If a person who shared in a particular event is still around, I try to get in touch with that person to ask about his or her memory of the event. Both of my brothers, Donald and Darrel, live close by, so I often ask them about an experience one or both of them shared with me when we were kids on the farm. Unfortunately, the older I get, the more difficult it is to find folks who were there at the time, as many of them have passed on. I often wish I could check with my mother or father about certain happenings that I remember so well. Thankfully, I interviewed both of them when they were in their eighties to capture some of their stories on my tape recorder.

In addition to consulting with others who remember the events I'm describing, I do research to verify facts, especially dates. I may remember a story very well, but I often can't recall the exact dates involved. For instance, I wrote a story about the celebration that occurred when Japan surrendered at the end of World War II. I had been at the free outdoor movie in Wild Rose when the news arrived. I heard shots fired and then saw American Legion members, World War I veterans, marching down Main Street and shooting their old army rifles into the air. People began yelling and cheering and tossing their caps in the air. "Our boys are coming home! Our boys are coming home!" they shouted. But I noticed one woman who was crying, not cheering. She was a Gold Star mother whose son had been killed in the war. He was not coming home. A little searching on the internet provided the date of that event: it was August 14, 1945, a Tuesday, that word spread around the world that Japan had surrendered.

Sometimes I encounter disagreement over the details of events. The same incident can be viewed quite differently by those who witnessed it. Once I wrote a story about how my two brothers and I were fishing with our father on Norwegian Lake, east of Wild Rose. We were using cane poles with earthworms for bait. We had caught several bluegills when Darrel's bobber dipped below the water's quiet surface and didn't return to the top. The cane pole bent and the fishing line tightened.

"You got a big one on," Pa said. "Maybe a northern, or could be a big bass. Grab your line so you don't break your pole."

Darrel grabbed the thick green line and began pulling as the rest of us watched. Ever so slowly, the big fish was coming to the surface. Except it wasn't a fish, it was an enormous snapping turtle. "Big as a washtub," Pa later described it.

"What do I do?" Darrel asked, a rather frightened look on his face. We all knew that snapping turtles could be dangerous.

"Cut the line," Pa said loudly, handing over his jackknife. Darrel cut the line and the huge turtle, with moss on its back, slowly settled back into the lake.

When I shared the story with my brothers many years later, Donald agreed with what I had written. "That's how I remember it," he said. Darrel looked up and said, "I wasn't even there. I was doing something else that day."

I had to make a decision. Do I include the story in the memoir I was writing, or leave it out? Deciding that a majority of us considered my version true, I included it in the book. I jokingly said later that I was lucky we had an odd number of children in my family. With an even number we would frequently end up with a tie, and I would have had to find another way of verifying stories.

13 Writing History

While a memoir relies largely on the writer's memories of the past, a history book is based entirely on fact and requires deep and thorough research. I have always enjoyed reading about history, hearing old-timers recount their histories, and watching TV and movies on history topics. Unfortunately, like many people, I found the history classes I took in high school to be deadly boring, as they mostly consisted of facts about people, places, and dates, all to be memorized and regurgitated on an examination.

Several of my early publications were books on history, from a history of my community of Wild Rose, *Village of Roses*, published in 1973, to *Barns of Wisconsin* and *Mills of Wisconsin and the Midwest* later in the 1970s. With each book I wrote in the history genre, I came to better understand that good storytelling is essential to keeping readers engaged and entertained—just as if they were reading a memoir or a novel. People are more likely to learn and retain historical facts if they enjoy the surrounding story.

Even for my history books, I tend to stay within my niche of writing on farming, small towns, and rural life.

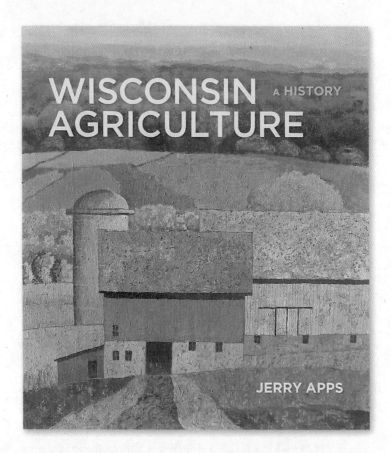

By following the age-old advice to "write what you know," I have plenty of stories to draw on when building story-telling elements into history narratives.

When considering my next history book project, I ask these questions: What do I already know about this topic? What has already been published on this topic? What are the questions I need to answer about the topic before I begin writing? What are the storytelling opportunities for this topic?

An example of this process is my book *Horse-Drawn Days: A Century of Farming with Horses*, published by the

Wisconsin Historical Society Press, publisher of many of
my histories. I was intrigued by an idea to write about the
history of horse-powered farm work. But before I wrote
a single word or did any research, I asked myself several
questions, beginning with the most obvious: What do I
already know about this topic? Having grown up driving
horses on the home farm, I had many stories and plenty
of personal experience with draft horses and horse-
drawn machinery. That was a start. I could fill more in
as I went.

Next, I did some mind mapping. I drew a circle in
the middle of a blank page and in it wrote, "Farming with
Horses." From the middle circle I drew lines to smaller
circles, where I wrote ideas about what to include in the
book: draft horse breeds, types of horse-drawn equipment, horse-related terminology, the years horses were
used in farming, and so on. This mind map became my
early guide to what I would include in the book, evolving
as I worked on the project.

Next I dug into "what I already know," recalling my
growing-up years on the farm when we used horses for all
of the heavy work. Here is a story I wrote about one of my
memories that became part of the book *Horse-Drawn Days*:

Frank and Charlie were Percheron draft horses,
brown with tan manes and tails, each weighing about
1,800 pounds. They were already members of my family, along with Fanny, our big brown and tan, long-
nosed collie, by the time I was born. When I was old
enough to be curious, I asked Pa how the horses got
their names. "We named them after our neighbors,
Frank Kolka and Charlie George," Pa said. People
living in a farm community knew the names of each

other's horses just as well as they knew the names of their kids. They knew the horses' personalities, too. For instance, our neighbor Wilbur Witt owned a horse named Jerry—a big, lazy, good-for-nothing animal that would kick or bite you every chance he got. Ma would never call me Jerry—it was always Jerold—because she didn't want anyone to compare me to the neighbor's worthless horse. . . .

Unlike the neighbor horse, Jerry, neither Frank nor Charlie ever tried to kick or bite me, but they did have some bad habits. By the time I was ten years old Pa showed me how to harness them. I was short for my age, so I had to stand on my tiptoes to toss the leather harness over their broad backs. When Pa was there watching, all went well. But Frank and Charlie knew when Pa wasn't around, and just before I tossed the harness onto either horse, he would squeeze me against the side of the stall—not hard enough to hurt me, but hard enough so I couldn't put the harness in place. I'd put down the harness, yell "get over" in my most authoritative ten-year-old voice, and slap the horse on the rump. The animal would move over, and I would continue harnessing him. This happened *every* time Pa was not around. It became a kind of game for Frank and Charlie and me, a sort of draft horse initiation for a farm kid growing up and learning the ways of horses and everything else on the farm. As I got older, taller, and stronger they no longer tried the "squeeze the kid" stunt nearly as often.

With my early memories captured, I made a second mind map. From a center circle labeled "research," I drew lines to circles where I wrote likely sources: "what I already know," "books and articles," "internet sources," "interview possibilities," and so on. I reviewed the newspaper archives available online at the Wisconsin Historical Society and made copies of relevant articles. I also researched books on the topic at the Wisconsin Historical Society Library and at Steenbock Library on the UW–Madison campus. When researching at the Wisconsin Historical Society, I learned that the archives there include the McCormick papers, a collection of correspondence, advertising materials, instruction manuals, and more related to the McCormick Company (later McCormick-Deering), one of the early and most prominent manufacturers of horse-drawn farm equipment. I spent many hours looking through this collection and taking notes.

On my Facebook page, I put out a request for people's stories about working with horses. I also sent a short piece to *The Country Today*, a newspaper for which I wrote two monthly columns, asking for draft-horse stories. I received numerous replies, several of which I included in the book. I spent about eighteen months researching the book, another year writing it, and about a year editing and rewriting.

Published in 2010, *Horse-Drawn Days* was my fourth book with the Wisconsin Historical Society Press. The first two, *Ringlingville USA* and the follow-up for children, *Tents, Tigers, and the Ringling Brothers*, had been based entirely on research, as I had no circus memories to incorporate. But starting with the 2008 publication of *Old Farm: A History*, I published a number of books with the WHS Press in which I wove together history and memories. In *Old Farm*, I recounted the history of our

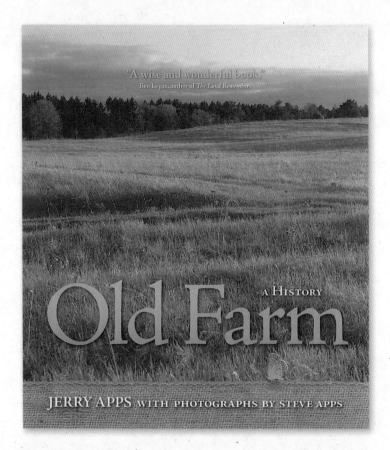

"A wise and wonderful book."
Ben Logan, author of *The Land Remembers*

A HISTORY

Old Farm

JERRY APPS WITH PHOTOGRAPHS BY STEVE APPS

family's 120-acre farm in Waushara County, from the glacier that formed the landscape to the Menominee Indians who lived on the land for hundreds of years to the succession of owners who had attempted to farm there. I also included archival photos, maps, and documents to make the book a historical documentation of our piece of land. But in addition, I described the activities of our family at the farm and shared my own perspectives on the importance of preserving the environment.

Certified Copy

CERTIFICATE OF MARRIAGE.

(To be returned within 30 days to the Register of Deeds of the County in which the license was issued.)

1. Full name of husband ... *Thomas J. Stewart*
2. Full name of father of husband ... *Solomon J. Stewart*
3. Full name of the mother of husband (a) ... *Sally Ann Stewart*
4. Occupation of husband ... *Farmer*
5. Residence of husband ... *Springwater*
6. Birthplace of husband ... *State of New York*
7. Full name of wife previous to marriage ... *Maria Jenks*
8. Full name of the father of wife ... *John T. Jenks*
9. Full name of the mother of wife (a) ... *Polly Jenks*
10. Birthplace of wife ...
11. The color of the parties (b) ... *White*
12. License, No. ... Date ...
13. Time when marriage was contracted ... *Aug 28th 1869*
14. The place, town or township, and county, where the marriage was contracted ... *Springwater*
15. By what ceremony contracted ...
16. Person signing certificate. ... *E. J. Davies*
    Person pronouncing marriage ... *E. J. Davies*
    Names of subscribing witnesses ...
    Date of Certificate ... *Aug 28th 1869*
17. Date of Registration *September 4th 1869*
    Any additional circumstances ...

PENSION U.S. OFFICE C MAY 14 1903

STATE OF WISCONSIN, }
Waushara County. } ss.
    I, C. F. Youngman, Register of Deeds, in and for said
County of Waushara, do hereby certify that I have compared the annexed copy of the original record in
my office and in my custody, and that the same is a correct transcript therefrom

of the Marriage of Thomas J. Stewart and Maria Jenks
    Witness my hand and the seal of said office, at Wantoma, Wisconsin,
this ... *8th* ... day of ... *May* ... 190 *3*.
    C. F. Youngman Register.
By ... Deputy.

(SEAL)

When researching my history books, I often use historic documents—
everything from maps, letters, catalog pages, patent registrations,
birth and death certificates, and other legal documents—as sources.
The marriage certificate of Tom Stewart, who homesteaded our farm
after his Civil War service, helped me tell the story of our land in *Old
Farm. Certificate of Marriage, Tom Stewart and Maria Jenks, Register of
Deeds, Waushara County, Wautoma, Wisconsin*

In the book's introduction I wrote:

> From land that provided only a marginal living for its
> early owners, this place we call Roshara has provided
> much for my family and me. Each year we harvest the
> bounty of our garden; gather wild grapes, plums and
> cherries for jelly; and cut a few trees for firewood to
> heat our cabin. . . . But far more significant than the
> material gifts are the spiritual ones we harvest from
> our farm during all seasons of the year. More than any-
> thing, these sandy acres, some wooded, some prairie,
> and some wetland, have enhanced our lives and given
> us new, richer perspectives about the land and all that
> it comprises.

As in *The Land Still Lives*, in *Old Farm* I combined writing
genres to create a hybrid that the publisher said "com-
bines history, memoir, and call to action."

To help me build the storytelling element in several
of my history books, I have reached out to the public to
invite them to share their stories, reminiscences, and
photographs as I did for *Horse-Drawn Days*. These books
include *Wisconsin Agriculture: A History*, *The Civilian Conservation Corps in Wisconsin: Nature's Army at Work*, *When
the White Pine Was King*, and *Meet Me on the Midway: A History of Wisconsin Fairs*.

For *Meet Me on the Midway*, I asked my contacts at
several of Wisconsin's agriculture newspapers if they
would print a short notice explaining that I was writing
a book about the history of Wisconsin's fairs and inviting
readers to share personal stories about their fair experiences. Almost immediately, the stories began rolling in:
stories about 4-H members and their calves, about judg-

ing exhibits or working in the food tents, about carnival workers, about meeting a future spouse at the fair. Humorous stories and sad stories. Stories about what fairs have meant to people. These memories breathe life into the facts and figures of history. Almost all of the stories came via email, and I followed up with questions and requests for more detail. I then wove many of the stories into my discussion of various fair history topics in *Meet Me on the Midway*, published by the Wisconsin Historical Society Press in 2022.

14 More Research Strategies

Some of my writing students roll their eyes when I bring up the topic of research. Some have even said, rather quietly, "We joined this workshop to learn about writing. What's with this research business?" I assure them that nearly everything I write requires research. For some book projects, I spend as much time, sometimes more, doing the research as I do writing the first draft. For me, nothing is more important than having a solid research base for writing.

As described in the last chapter, I start the research process right from the idea stage to help me determine what topics to pursue. Although I have spent countless hours researching in libraries, archives, and newspaper archives (sometimes called morgues), these days I am able to do a surprising amount of research on the internet. For my book *Horse-Drawn Days*, for example, I searched online for current and historical articles related to farming with draft horses. I printed those that seemed promising and put them in my research file.

An important consideration when doing research on the internet is determining if the source of the information is credible. Generally speaking, universities and historical societies and their staff and faculty are reliable, accurate sources. Even for these sources, I usually dig deeper to assess the quality. Who wrote the piece—student, professor, someone else—and what are their credentials? For topics that are complicated or controversial, such as climate change, I look for multiple sources, especially if there is disagreement among sources. Sometimes, when there is no clear single answer, I share the several perspectives that I uncover.

Interviews are another important research tactic for much of my work. I make a list of people I know or learn about in my research who might have information or stories to share on the topic. Then I reach out to them, explain my project, and request an interview. I prefer to interview in person, but when that is not possible I interview by phone. I record every interview using a tiny digital recorder with an excellent microphone so I can rest it on the table rather than sticking it in front of the person's face. This recorder also allows me to interview over the telephone and capture both my questions and the responses. Occasionally I will email my questions in advance, especially if I am looking for specific dates and events that the person may want to look up before talking with me. But I prefer not sending the questions ahead to produce more candid answers.

I make sure to ask at the beginning of an interview if it's okay to record the conversation, saying something like, "I want to make sure that when I write about what you've said, I get it right." I've never had an interview subject say no to recording an interview. If it is a long and complicated interview, I may email the person my written transcription of what they said.

I've been interviewing people since my days as a high school newspaper editor, and I've picked up some tips along the way. I memorize my questions so I don't have to read them from a piece of paper, and I try to be as informal as possible. I've learned to be patient and listen. I ask a question, and then I shut up. I allow the person to take a moment or two before answering—I don't rush it. If the person seems to wander away from the answer I expected, I let it happen. This often leads to information that is more interesting and more important than what I was looking for. Most important, I do not interrupt if the person begins telling a story related to the question. I am always looking for good stories.

I've learned to ask at the end of the interview, "Is there anything you'd like to tell me that I haven't asked?" I almost always get more. And I have learned to keep the recorder running after I have thanked the person and am packing up to leave. Often the most interesting material comes after my more formal questioning ends.

I've had my share of problems and challenges when interviewing. Once I was interviewing a barrel maker for *Breweries of Wisconsin*. He began telling me about how busy he was during Prohibition, when all the breweries and taverns were closed. In the middle of his story about doing some work for Al Capone, his wife chimed in, "Don't tell him about that!" Thankfully he kept talking, reminding his wife he doubted he'd be arrested these many years later. Since then I try to interview people without others present.

Occasionally, an interview subject has insisted on answering my questions with only "yes" or "no" answers. I learned to prepare questions where such answers cannot be given, such as: "What do you remember about . . ." or "Exactly how did that machine work?" This strategy is especially helpful when I am interviewing on the phone.

After an interview, I plug my digital recorder into my computer, where I listen to the interview and begin typing the transcript. As I type I do some editing, not changing any details or meaning, just getting rid of the "*ahs*," "*you knows*," and repetition.

I also conduct informal interviews by email. When I wrote the history of fairs in Wisconsin, I searched online to find each county fair manager's email address. Then I emailed the manager asking for information about the fair's history, when it first opened, changes over the years, and so on. About half of the fair managers were able to provide this information. Some referred me to a local historical society, and I sent a new round of emails with my questions. I was able to fill in much of the basic information about each fair using this method.

Early on in my writing career, I learned the importance of having a filing system for the research material I accumulate. Nothing frustrates me more than trying to find a fact or quote that I know I have but can't locate. For some books, I have as many as four hundred pieces of research. It would be an impossible task to find something without a system. I give a number to every piece of research—whether it is a story someone emailed me, an article I found online and printed, the transcript of an interview, or a book I consulted. I record this list of numbered materials in a file on my computer, with a description of the source and a few key words that I can use for a computer search. For every piece of research I uncover, I am also careful to record its source, no matter if it is a book or a website. I have never been accused of plagiarism, but I nevertheless always want to be prepared to show proper attribution for my research findings. I file the paper version of each research item in a file folder, in numerical order, and place it in a portable filing box.

As I write, I almost always discover that I need to do more research on a given topic. For example, when I began writing *Horse-Drawn Days*, I knew that draft horses had ushered in a revolutionary change in farming, but I discovered that I needed to include information about how farmers farmed before draft horses. The answer, of course, was human power and oxen. So I stopped writing and went back to research. I learned that in the early days of wheat growing in Wisconsin, farmers planted wheat seeds by hand, cut the ripe wheat with a cradle (a form of scythe) by hand, gathered the cut wheat into bundles by hand, hauled the wheat to a three-bay threshing barn on ox carts, and threshed the grain by laying it on the barn floor and pounding it with a flail—or sometimes by having an ox walk over the grain. These research findings helped me tell a more complete history and produce a better book.

15 Return to Fiction

Even after I set aside my dreams of writing fiction to concentrate on memoirs and history books, every so often, a
little voice in the back of my mind would ask, When are
you going to try writing another novel?

It was on my annual canoe trip to the Boundary Waters of northern Minnesota with my son Steve in 1999
that the topic of writing a novel came up again. I was now
sixty-five years old. Steve has always been a good sound-
ing board for my writing ideas. Sitting by a smoky campfire, on a clear, star-studded night, with a loon calling
in the distance, we began talking about a potential novel.

Back in 1972, I had written a history of my hometown,
Village of Roses, for the Wild Rose Historical Society. It
was while writing that book that I had learned about an
unusual religious group, the Standalones, who had come
to Wild Rose from upper New York State in the 1850s.
One of their tenets was that each person had a right to
believe whatever he or she wanted and not be tied to
any doctrine. The Standalones did not have a religious
leader—no pastor, preacher, or priest. At the time, Wild
Rose had Baptist, Methodist, and Presbyterian churches.
The Standalones were clearly an anomaly.

As we talked, I began to think about a couple of other subjects I was curious about and wondered whether I could make them part of a story about a group like the Standalones. I had long been interested in the medicine show men who traveled by horse and wagon and sold elixirs that cured "whatever ails you." And, since high school, I had been interested in soil conservation and had even written an original oration on the topic titled "The Hole in Uncle Sam's Pocket."

I asked Steve what he thought about a novel that would feature the Standalones, but with a religious leader who also was a medicine show man who traveled the Midwest selling a special elixir as he promoted the need for soil conservation. Steve said he thought the idea had possibility.

Back in Madison, daughter Sue also said the idea had promise. Ruth was less positive. I continued thinking about the idea, giving my main character the name Increase Joseph Link. "Increase" came from Increase Lapham, one of Wisconsin's early researchers and authors. "Joseph Link" just seemed to go well with Increase. On August 15, 2000, I wrote this in my journal:

I am working on my novel and I have several big problems. How do I frame the main character, Increase Joseph Link, so he is taken seriously, yet is clearly eccentric and does unusual, unexpected things? In my early draft, I am afraid I have him looking goofy, which destroys his credibility. How do I describe the religion he founded so it sounds plausible, yet is clearly different from other known religions in the community?

I slogged on with the novel, taking breaks from time to time to work on my nonfiction writing. The story was coming together slowly as I tried to weave together the antics of Increase Joseph, his unusual church, and his concern for soil conservation.

Nearly a year later, in July 2001, I wrote this in my journal:

> Working on Increase Joseph Link book. Great fun. For the Standalone Fellowship, I have created a round church, or maybe it should be octagonal. So far, Ruth has not warmed up to the novel. She thinks the entire book, as I have it so far, is one step away from, or maybe right in the middle of being completely stupid. She may be right.

By late 2002, I had completed yet another draft of the novel, now with the title *The Land Comes First*. I shared the manuscript with various family members, including Matt Apps, my nephew, who lived with us for five years while he attended the University of Wisconsin–Madison. On December 21, 2002, I wrote in my journal:

> Matt came by the house this evening. He thinks my Increase Joseph book is my best writing yet. Ruth is still not convinced of its merits. Next, I'll ask Sue to read it and offer her opinion. Matt also offered several good suggestions for revision.

I believed that the manuscript for *The Land Comes First* was far enough along that I should begin looking for a publisher. I knew I would have no luck landing a New

York publisher without the help of an agent, so I began looking for a regional press. Through Steve I knew Marv Balousek, a reporter for the *Wisconsin State Journal*, who owned a small publishing house in Madison called Badger Books and served as its primary editor. He also wrote books.

I had lunch with Marv and agreed to send him a proposal along with seven chapters of what I was still calling *The Land Comes First*. In my journal on January 14, 2003, I wrote:

> Steve and Matt think it's a good book. I'll wait and see what Marv thinks. I've been working on this novel off and on since 1999. Be fun to see it in print. I have about 100 plus pages in draft. I am planning on about 250 pages.

On January 26, I wrote:

> No word from Badger Books. I have 140 pages of draft manuscript. Good chance they will turn it down because it strays some distance from my quite successful books, *Barns of Wisconsin* and *Rural Wisdom*, each having sold so far more 25,000 copies. It comes down to how much faith I have in the book.

I heard from Marv on February 1. He liked what he had seen and wanted to see the completed manuscript. I finished the first draft on February 17, with March and April set aside for revisions. Marv was not thrilled with my working title, so Sue, Steve, Ruth, and I came up with a new title: *The Travels of Increase Joseph*. I sent the final manuscript, now 260 pages, off to Badger Books on

April 12 and heard from them a month later: they would publish my novel. I wrote in my journal on May 28, 2003:

> James Michener complained he was 40 years old before he published his first novel. I will be 69. I did manage to publish my first book, albeit nonfiction in 1970, when I was 36.

On November 3, 2003, we launched the novel at Barnes & Noble in Madison. About 125 people attended, and we sold fifty copies of the book, plus another sixty copies of my backlist books.

Shortly thereafter, reviews started appearing. One reviewer wrote, "Humorous history with a contemporary application." Another said, "Increase Joseph was an ecologist before his time. He insisted that the land was sacred, that clear cutting forests was wrong, and that people ought to love one another." A third wrote, "Apps has put together a history of life and farming in the last half of the 19th century, beginning when farming was in its most basic form and ending with the coming of electricity." I was surprised and elated. The reviews were much stronger than I expected.

I was indebted to Marv for taking a chance on my "quirky" novel and giving me the confidence I needed to publish other fiction. Buoyed by the positive reviews for *The Travels of Increase Joseph*, I began thinking about a follow-up. How could I build on the successes of *Increase*? Was there another rural issue, similar to soil conservation, that I could build a good story around?

I had long been concerned about the demise of the small family farm, which had begun disappearing following World War II. Could I write a novel that would help readers understand what was being lost when fewer and fewer people lived on and farmed the land? While I was considering this, Susan reminded me that I had shared many stories with the family about the four summers I had managed a cucumber-salting station. Could those stories be the basis for a novel?

The result was *In a Pickle*, published by the University of Wisconsin Press in 2007. Several more novels followed, each tackling an issue related to the future of farming and land conservation and all published by the UW Press: *Blue Shadows Farm*, on land use planning, in 2007; *Cranberry Red*, on food safety, in 2010; *Tamarack River Ghost*, on the challenges of industrial farming, in 2012; *The Great Sand Fracas of Ames County*, on the problems posed by sand mining for the oil-fracking industry, in 2014; *Cold as Thunder*, on climate change, in 2018. The most recent, *Settlers Valley*, tells the story of a group of disabled military veterans who take up small-acreage farming with the intent of working the land as a way of healing.

All that time, another project had lain restlessly on my shelf. Every two or three years, I dusted off the manuscript for *The Wild Oak* and then put it aside again as other publishing opportunities came along. Finally, in 2019, after seeing some success with my novels for adults, I asked Susan to take a look at the *Wild Oak* manuscript. By this time Sue was a published author of a children's book, and she made many excellent suggestions for revising the book, including excluding some characters and adding a new one. I spent a couple of months revising the manuscript one more time. In 2021, nearly forty years after I had written the first draft, Three Towers Press published *The Wild Oak*.

Courtesy of the
University of
Wisconsin Press

Courtesy of
HenschelHAUS
Publishing

16 Agents and Publishers

A literary agent represents authors' interests by pitching books to publishers. They also represent authors in contract negotiations and help ensure the author gets the best deal financially. For this service, an agent usually receives a percentage of the author's income as a royalty (agents are never paid upfront). Agents can be helpful—necessary, even—for those who want to see their work published by one of the country's large trade publishers, all of them based in New York, as many large presses won't consider unagented manuscripts.

By the 1980s, I had published several academic and trade books without an agent. From 1976 to 1982, I had worked part-time for the McGraw-Hill Book Company, College Division, as an acquisitions/consulting editor. McGraw also published three of my academic books. By that time, I had learned a good deal about the publishing industry and had concluded that if any of my books were to be published by a New York publisher, I would need an agent.

From the mid-1980s to 1999, I worked with three literary agents. Although they are often spoken about as though they hold all the secrets to getting published, agents are humans and sometimes make mistakes. Their opinions are subjective, just like anyone's. The first one I worked with, whose name I will not reveal, was suggested to me by my writing mentor, Bob Gard. I signed a contract with this agent in 1986 and worked with him for more than a year. He was not successful in negotiating any deals with publishers for me. In a July 25, 1987, letter to him I wrote, "It has been a month since we've talked, so I thought I best put some things in writing. We have worked together formally for nine months and more than a year informally. So, it is time to do an assessment. . . . Unless you've heard from some publisher in the past few weeks, I see absolutely no results in the past 12 months. Not one contract, not one letter of interest that might lead to a contract." I went on to explain in detail the books I was working on and that I was hoping he was sending around to potential publishers—which, apparently, he was not doing. I hired an attorney in August 1987 to help me terminate the agreement.

My second agent, with whom I had an informal relationship, I will also keep anonymous. I submitted my manuscript for *Rural Wisdom* to her, and she told me that nobody would buy that kind of book. Amherst Press eventually published the book and it became one of my best sellers. I didn't share any more of my writing with her.

My most productive agent relationship was with the Larry Sternig Literary Agency from the late 1980s until 1999, when Larry passed away. Larry tried very hard to find a New York publisher for my books. His passing was a great loss.

For several years I continued looking for an agent. In my journal on January 2, 2001, I wrote:

I'm still smarting a little from another literary agent turndown. A representative of the literary agency I had contacted wrote:

"Your work strikes me as being outside of our current focus of highly commercial fiction and nonfiction for the general trade market."

My writing is about rural life, rural history, and country living that I think interests many people. What all of this means is I must discover a new way of finding publishers and promoting my work.

And that's what I did. I quit searching for an agent and struck out on my own, learning how to work directly with publishers. When seeking a publisher, I begin with research, just as I do for a writing project. I look online for publishers that have published on the topic I am writing about. (Publishers who have never published in my subject area are unlikely to want to start now.) I have worked with publishers of every size and almost every type, the exception is vanity presses, more commonly known today as self-publishers. I confess that I have a soft place in my heart for regional publishers. The advantages are many: I've enjoyed meeting with editors and marketing people and getting to know them on a personal basis. I also believe they can more easily adjust to societal changes and ever-changing marketing conditions than the giant New York presses can. I would compare regional publishers to nimble motorboats that can turn on a dime when they face a challenging situation, while the large conglomerates are like cruise ships that take a mile or more just to stop.

I've seen some disadvantages in working with small regional publishers, as well. The smallest ones, those with only a handful of staff, often do not have the resources to do the marketing required for most books to be successful on a large scale. Some small presses also have a hard time getting the attention of retailers and reviewers.

It is understandable that a frustrated book author might look to one of the many self-publishing opportunities now available. Of course, self-publishing usually means the author must bear some or all of the costs of producing the book and is often left to handle all the marketing and promotions on their own. But it can be a good option for an author with a good story to tell who has been unsuccessful getting a contract with a traditional press or who wants to retain creative control of both their work and any profits. Several of my writing students have gone this route with good results.

Almost all publisher websites include a set of submission guidelines that describe what they are looking for and explain how to submit a query or proposal. I have found that it is important to follow those guidelines, or I risk never receiving a response. Here are the submission guidelines for the University of Wisconsin Press, a publisher I have worked with frequently:

> To inquire about potential interest in your project, you may submit a brief e-mail query of 1–3 paragraphs describing your project, or you may proceed directly to a proposal. Do not submit a whole manuscript unless an editor invites it. If someone has referred you to the University of Wisconsin Press, or if you are approaching our editors as a follow-up to a conversation with our staff at a conference or other event, please be sure to mention this connection in your first contact with us.

THE REVIEW PROCESS

Once we receive your materials, we will review them carefully. If your project is a good fit for our list, we will notify you of our interest and request any additional materials.

Owing to the sheer volume of proposals we receive; it may take up to four months for us to respond. During the waiting period, our editors do not accept phone queries regarding the status of your proposal, but please feel free to send a follow-up query via email.

When approaching any publisher, I first write a query letter to the acquisitions editor. I say enough about the book to convince her that she would want to see a book proposal. With a positive response to my query letter, I begin working on a book proposal, following the publisher's proposal guidelines.

Most of the publishers I work with ask for similar information in their proposal forms: percentage of text complete and expected completion date, target word and illustration counts, research approach, outline of the content, synopsis of each chapter, intended audience, competing titles already on the market, and why my project is the right fit for them. They also request sample writing from the book—usually a chapter or two or, in the case of fiction, the full manuscript. For all of my books, I have already done considerable work before submitting a proposal; for nonfiction books, I try to have 10 to 20 percent of a rough draft prepared before I develop the proposal. I usually give myself about a year out from the date of the proposal as the date that I plan to turn in the manuscript.

Developing a comprehensive book proposal has always been a challenging task for me, but a necessary one. Decision makers at the press need to answer such basic questions as, Is there a market for this book? Does this author have the qualifications needed to write this book? Does the book have a focus, a major theme? Does the research plan for the book appear to be doable? Are the writing samples well written, informative, interesting? Does the writing timeline suggested by the author appear reasonable—is the author giving himself or herself enough time to do the necessary research and write the book?

The publisher uses this preliminary information, along with a number of other factors, to begin to form a vision for the book that includes such decisions as page count, trim size, hardcover versus paperback format, whether to print in color or black and white, and so on. The acquisitions editor consults with others at the publishing house—marketing, editorial, production, and the business office—to discuss many facets of the proposal, including how well it fits the publishing house's list and mission and how well it is likely to sell. Some publishing houses submit new proposals to an editorial review committee for their buy-in as well. That decision-making process can take many months—sometimes a year or longer. While my proposal is being considered, I might hear back from the acquisitions editor with questions or suggestions, and I might be asked to revise the material or provide more text. These preliminary discussions also result in an early budget that helps the publisher decide whether to offer me a contract.

A book contract is a legally binding document between the author and the publisher (and in some cases, the agent). Each contract contains a series of paragraphs and subparagraphs outlining the specifics of the agreement, many of which can be negotiated.

Here are some of the common elements in a typical book contract:

Grant of Rights. Here the author grants the rights to the publisher to publish the work, usually "in all forms and media." This means print, audiobooks, and ebooks. This paragraph can also refer to translation rights and specify the "territories," or parts of the world, where the publisher can sell the book.

Delivery and Publication. This paragraph includes details about word count and delivery date. Typical language includes, "The author shall deliver to the publisher an electronic version of the complete Work in an approved software format." If illustrations are to be included in the book, a statement about the form in which they are submitted is included here. Several other items can appear here as well, such as the book title and the author's agreement to read and correct proofs.

Copyright. This section defines who holds copyright in the material to be used in the published work and who will register the copyright information with the Library of Congress, the body that maintains US copyright records. (I negotiate to retain copyright in my material.)

Permission Fees. Here the contract outlines the details related to who will obtain any necessary permissions for use of text or images. My contracts state that I, as the author, am responsible for permissions. For example, if I want to use a photograph owned by someone else, I will need to ask permission from the copyright holder and likely pay a licensing fee.

Representations, Warranties, and Indemnities. The author certifies ownership of the work, that it is original and contains no "scandalous, obscene, or libelous" material. This paragraph also contains details about actions that will be taken if a legal claim is filed against the publisher.

Termination. Look here for an outline of the steps that will be taken by the publisher if the author fails to meet delivery deadlines or the author fails to make changes to the work as recommended by the publisher.

Royalties. Royalties refer to the percentage of the book's net revenue or list price that will be paid to the author. This is one of the paragraphs most often negotiated.

Statements and Payment. The publisher indicates when and how often royalty statements and payments will be sent to the author—quarterly, every six months, or annually.

Subsidiary Rights. This paragraph covers matters related to the sale of subsidiary rights in the work, such as film, serial, or anthology rights. Generally the author receives 50 percent of the net amount received by the publisher for the licensing of these rights.

Book contracts often include additional paragraphs related to revisions, promotion and publicity, author's gratis copies (I usually receive ten free copies), what happens when the book goes out of print, and a noncompetition clause, in which the author agrees not to publish anything of similar character with another publisher. (Book contracts are complicated documents to wade through, especially for new authors. For more information, visit www.morse.law/news/book-publishing -contracts or www.authorsguild.org.)

After negotiations are complete and the contract finalized, the document is signed by a publisher representative and the author. Many authors celebrate this moment. Since writing books has been my job for the past twenty-five years, I've done my share of celebrating, but these days I am simply ready to get back to work on the project.

With a signed contract in hand, I continue to revise the manuscript, with the goal of delivering all materials to the publisher on or before the deadline specified in the contract. Aside from the occasional break in writing to do more research, I plug along, writing and working toward that delivery date.

Having a delivery date can be a great motivator for completing a draft. Some years ago, a student in one of my writing workshops was working on her memoir. When she completed a draft of the first paragraph, she began revising and rewriting. She wrote and rewrote and rewrote some more. When she returned to my workshop a year later, I told her I was looking forward to reading a draft of her memoir.

"Oh, I don't have a draft. But I think I've got the first paragraph absolutely perfect," she said.

I didn't have the heart to tell her that during the editing process, that paragraph was likely to be revised—or completely replaced.

17 The Editing Process

For some writers, editing and revising their work is drudgery. I have come to value and even enjoy the process. I begin by setting aside a completed draft manuscript to rest for several weeks. I tell my writing students, "I'm allowing the manuscript to ferment."

When I return to the manuscript after its fermenting time, I come to it with fresh ideas. I read the manuscript all the way through without stopping. Then I take a few minutes to reflect on what I've just read, and, recalling the question put to me long ago by a New York editor, I ask myself, "What is this book about?" I write out the answer and tape it alongside my computer—and then I read the manuscript once more, slowly and deliberately. If I find a sentence, a paragraph, sometimes an entire chapter that does not relate to what I think the book is about, I take it out. Likewise, as I read I mark any places where I need to add more to better demonstrate what the book is about. Often this means I must do additional research, perhaps conduct another interview or two, read a research report—whatever it takes to strengthen the main theme of the book.

After I do this additional research and writing, I consider again whether I have the chapters in the right order. Do they follow a logical sequence, each contributing to the main theme? For my fiction manuscripts, I make sure the elements of a good story are present: a compelling beginning, middle, and end; interesting characters who readers can picture and who have a real reason for being there; a clearly drawn time and place; action to propel the story; a strong central conflict; and enough suspense to keep the reader reading.

At this stage in the editing process, I turn the manuscript over to Ruth. She is already familiar with the content, having reviewed the early stages of my writing before I even submitted a book proposal. Now she reads the completed manuscript and writes comments. Depending on the topic, I may also ask one or more of my children to read and comment.

With all this family input, I make one more round of changes in the manuscript before I begin my final step, searching for any spelling and grammatical errors. If I have included footnotes, I double-check to make sure they are complete and accurate. When I've finished this step, I make sure that the file on my computer is the most recent, corrected one (I also keep all of the working files in case I have to go back to review something in an earlier draft). I send the completed draft to my publisher, always in advance of the date in the contract. These days I send the materials as email attachments, but for many years, I sent completed manuscripts through the mail.

Even though the manuscript I've just delivered has been through many rounds of editing by me, Ruth, and other family members, the editing has just begun. My acquisitions editor reviews my submission to ensure I have met my contractual obligations and may request some preliminary revisions or additions. From there, the manuscript will move through several phases of professional editing before it is typeset in pages.

Several of my writing students have self-published books, and some of them consider themselves better than average editors. I often hear, "Oh, my Aunt Ethyl is a retired English teacher, I'll get her to read it," or "My cousin John writes a column for the local weekly newspaper, I'll ask him to look at it." These people can offer valuable tips for improving manuscripts—but they are not professional editors. Experienced editors have the tools and the training to ask questions and suggest where to find the answers. They understand book publishing conventions and the best practices for the different genres in which they specialize. They also know when to break the rules.

In the early days of my writing career, I was often put out by editorial queries—hadn't I and my own text reviewers done a reasonable job of editing? I soon came to realize that editors were not the enemy. They were on my side, helping to make my work as good as it could possibly be.

After my manuscript has made its way into the press's editorial pipeline, I hear from the developmental editor who has been assigned to work on the book. (Depending on the size of the publishing firm, the acquisitions editor may also serve as my developmental editor.) The developmental editor begins by taking a "big-picture" look at the manuscript's structure. She looks for logic in the book's presentation, determines what is missing and what is extraneous, considers whether the chapters are in the best order, and evaluates whether some chapters or sections can be combined and others dropped.

I receive a series of queries from the developmental editor requesting my approval of changes she has made in the manuscript and asking me to rewrite certain sections or sentences to sharpen the focus, provide more detail, clear up inconsistencies, and improve transitions. Many developmental editors also edit to correct grammar and spelling.

For illustrated books, the developmental editor helps plan and create the images that will appear in the finished product. In addition to images I provide, she often suggests additional photos or illustrations to help support the text and underscore the points I am making in the book. She also helps create the captions for the images. Additionally, especially at small presses, the developmental editor helps select the cover design, writes copy for the cover and catalog, and requests blurbs from people who can help promote the book. I have been fortunate that with most of my publishers, I have a say in what the cover will look like, although the publisher makes the final decision.

Responding to the developmental editors' questions can take many hours of work. As an example, for one of my agriculture history books, I kept a record of the days and hours I spent responding to revisions by the developmental editor. For an eighty-thousand-word manuscript, I spent parts of twelve days (forty-five hours) responding to suggestions and questions.

At some presses, including the Wisconsin Historical Society Press, the developmental editor or an editorial assistant fact-checks manuscripts, checking sources, verifying citations and website addresses, and making sure that dates, places, and references to people are accurate. For my book *Wisconsin Agriculture: A History*, the fact-checker pointed out that a person I was quoting had died two years before the date of the quote. Fact-checkers save authors (and publishers) from publishing such embarrassments.

After I have responded to the developmental editor's and the fact-checker's comments, suggestions, and questions, the manuscript goes to a copyeditor, who reviews the material for consistency, spelling and grammatical errors, and adherence to language style rules. Later, when the book is typeset into pages, it's reviewed for any lingering errors by the last line of defense: a proofreader.

Over many years and many books, I've increasingly come to appreciate the good work editors do in preparing my work for publication. It can be a little ego bruising, but I've learned that it's the collaboration between author and editor that can make the difference between producing a mediocre book and one that is exceptional.

18 Writing for Children and Young Adults

Although I had started writing a novel in 1982 that was eventually published for young readers in 2021, for most of my career I had no aspirations to write children's picture books. I considered it a highly specialized form of writing, and I wasn't sure I had either the knowledge or the skills necessary.

Then, in July 1999, during a noon gathering of students at the School of the Arts at Rhinelander, I read from my book *When Chores Were Done*. One of the stories was about the time we grew several acres of rutabagas when I was a kid on the farm. After my talk, one of my fellow writing instructors said to me, "Jerry, you should write a children's book about your rutabaga experience."

I took the idea to Amherst Press, publisher of *When Chores Were Done*, where the original rutabaga story had appeared. They agreed to publish it, with a color illustration on each page. Now I had to figure out how I would write it. After a lot of work, including studying children's picture books and reflecting on how they were done, and several conversations with the artist Amherst Press selected, Annika Beatty-Andersen, the children's hardcover picture book *Eat Rutabagas* came out in 2002. It was followed by a second one, *Stormy*, about my 4-H calf, later that year.

Also in 1999, I began thinking about writing a book for young adults about what farm life was like when I was a kid. I considered writing it in the form of fictional letters a young lad wrote to his grandmother about life on the farm during the Depression years of the 1930s. In a June 12, 1999, entry in my journal, I reported that I had three chapters in draft. "Will keep working on it." I was tentatively titling it *Letters to Grandma*.

In between talks, book signings, and other writing commitments, by August 6, 1999, I had completed ninety-nine pages of a first rough draft of *Letters to Grandma*. As happens with all of my writing at this stage, my internal judging self began to nag at me. I wrote in my journal, "As usual, I have so many concerns. Is this work as terrible as it seems? Will any publisher want to publish it? Will anybody buy it if it is published? I will keep plugging along. I've only about 15 to 20 pages to go and I'll have a first draft finished."

On September 17, I wrote: "I have been revising my young adult's book, I'm now calling it 'Letters from Hillside Farm.' I'm working on chapter nine; each chapter is only a few pages long. I wonder what some editor will think of it—always a concern when I launch into a new area of writing (for me)."

I shared the finished manuscript with several young-reader publishers. I received encouraging words, but no contract. The manuscript sat on the shelf in my office, gathering dust along with other unpublished works.

In 2004, the Wisconsin Historical Society Press had published my history of the Ringling Brothers Circus, *Ringlingville USA*. A couple of years later, Bobbie Malone of the Wisconsin Historical Society's Office of

School Services asked if I would be interested in writing a children's book on the same topic for the WHS Press's Badger Biographies Series. After some discussion about the approach—it would be much shorter than the adult version, with lots of photos and a glossary of circus terms—I agreed to do it. Bobbie and other WHS Press editors helped make sure the text was appropriate for the age level, with shorter sentences and simpler vocabulary than I included in *Ringlingville USA*. Here is a brief excerpt:

> The Ringling boys heard the steam whistle of the riverboat before they could see it paddling up the river. The whistle meant visitors were coming to town. Growing up in McGregor, Iowa, on the Mississippi River, the boys had seen many riverboats. Steam engines powered these huge boats. Some of them were 3 or 4 stories tall and 250 feet long. . . . By 1869, there were seven Ringling Boys. At 16, Al was the oldest, with Gus just a year younger. Otto was 11, and then followed the four youngest brothers: six-year-old Alf T., four-year-old Charles, and three-year-old John. Baby Henry was not even a year old. . . . When the Ringling boys heard the steamboat's whistle blow, all but baby Henry hurried to the McGregor boat landing. Many riverboats stopped in McGregor, but one day in 1869 it was a circus boat. A circus riverboat was special.

Tents, Tigers, and the Ringling Brothers was published in 2006. Not long after, Bobbie Malone contacted me again to ask, "Would you be interested in writing another book for the WHS Press Badger Biographies Series?" She had seen my book *Cheese: The Making of a Wisconsin Tradition*, published by the University of Wisconsin Press in 1998,

and she knew a story about a Swiss cheese maker in Green County named Casper Jaggi. To write the book, I would have to do considerable research. I had written about Swiss cheese making in Green County in the UW Press book, but I knew nothing about Casper Jaggi. With the help of Jaggi's son Fritz and others, I stitched together the book, which was published in 2008. I focused on Casper, but I also wrote about the history of cheese making in Wisconsin. I included chapters on how Swiss cheese is made and what life was like growing up in a cheese factory. I included a glossary of cheese-making terms, plus discussion questions and activities for young readers.

In 2010, I began writing my first book for Fulcrum Publishing, *Campfires and Loon Calls*. Examining their backlist one day, I noticed that they had published a few novels. Almost on a whim, I submitted my young adult novel *Letters from Hillside Farm* to Fulcrum. They published it in 2012—only thirteen years after I wrote it.

I have also been pleased to learn that young adults read my memoirs, most frequently *Whispers and Shadows*, *Never Curse the Rain*, *The Quiet Season*, and *Simple Things: Lessons from the Family Farm*. Young people seem especially interested in what it was like growing up on a farm during the Great Depression and World War II, when my family had no electricity or indoor plumbing and I attended a one-room country school. I have been a teacher for many years, and I'm pleased to continue to teach through my books.

19 Teaching Writing

I have degrees in teaching, and I have taught since 1957. But I do not have a degree in journalism, English, or creative writing, and my formal training in how to write is thin: a few noncredit courses, a couple of workshops, and a shelf of books on the topic of creative writing. And so I was surprised when, a year after the publication of my first book, *The Land Still Lives*, in 1970, my writing mentor Robert E. Gard asked me to teach a two-week workshop at the School of the Arts at Rhinelander. I had attended the workshop as a student back in the mid-1960s and had a good deal of respect for the program. But I had never dreamed of teaching there. I eagerly said yes. I began teaching at SOA, as it was popularly known, in 1971 and did so for thirty-two years.

Professor Gard, a faculty member of the University of Wisconsin–Madison, founded this noncredit, two-week (later one-week) workshop in 1964. In its early years it focused solely on writing. Gard's friend L. G. Sorden, who had been a university extension agent in Oneida County, located in Wisconsin's North Woods, helped Gard organize the workshop in Rhinelander. The first one attracted fifty students along with six writing

instructors. As the years passed, SOA added instructors
with other artistic interests. By 1973, the school offered
classes in fiction writing, poetry writing, playwriting,
writing for children, article writing, music, dance, creative drama, and painting.

For the 1973 School
of the Arts session,
I taught a class on
article writing.
According to my bio
in the brochure, I
was then the author
of three books
and wrote two
weekly newspaper
columns on "nature
appreciation."

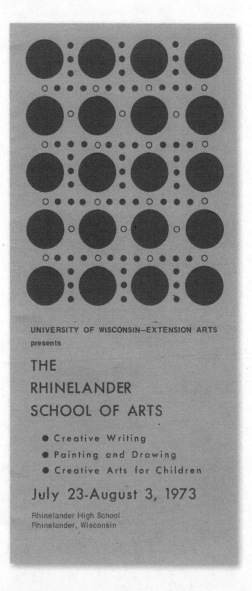

UNIVERSITY OF WISCONSIN—EXTENSION ARTS
presents

THE
RHINELANDER
SCHOOL OF ARTS

- Creative Writing
- Painting and Drawing
- Creative Arts for Children

July 23-August 3, 1973

Rhinelander High School
Rhinelander, Wisconsin

I have many stories from the years I taught at SOA. One year, a young man who had enrolled in my workshop took me aside during a break. He said, "I have a story I am working on, but I would ask that you sign this form, saying that you will not use my idea for your writing."

I said, "I don't steal students' ideas, but I will sign the form for you. And by the way, what are you planning to write about?" I was assuming the young fellow had a powerful story idea. I couldn't believe what he told me. "I'm working on a consumer's guide to houses of prostitution in Nevada," he said. "I've already done some preliminary research."

With a straight face—or as close to a straight face as I could muster—I said, "I'll sign your form and promise not to steal your idea." I never heard how far he got with his book.

I felt fortunate to be teaching with instructors who had won national awards and acclaim. I got to know them during the evenings, when the instructors got together for a variety of social events. To many of the students, however, I looked like just another one of them. Walking around the high school where the classes were held, instead of questions about writing, I was often asked, "Say, do you happen to know where the restroom is?" These questions kept me humble.

In the years I taught at SOA, my students included farmers, schoolteachers, attorneys, factory workers, retirees, students in their late teens, students in their late eighties—all interested in putting words down on paper. My role there required me to do lots of research and reading about how to teach everything from article writing to nonfiction book writing, memoir writing, and storytelling. I was learning as I was teaching—probably learning more than the students I was teaching.

The School of the Arts attracted many nationally known writers as instructors over the years, including Pulitzer Prize winner Archibald MacLeish, Dale Wasserman, Henry Mark Petrakis, Studs Terkel, Robert Bly, and Jesse Stuart. After more than a fifty-year run, the school ceased operations in 2015. Bob Gard's philosophy for the school was one that I appreciated and applauded. He said, "The arts are for everyone, no matter what your income level, where you lived, and how much education you had." The School of the Arts at Rhinelander was a laboratory for that philosophy.

Mark Lefebvre, a longtime friend of Gard's and one-time president of the Madison publisher Stanton & Lee, said this about the School of the Arts when he learned of its closing:

> I broke down and cried. I thought of the many summers I spent with Bob at the School of the Arts. I think of all the people whose lives were awakened. I think of the extraordinary faculty who in that very special place made real magic happen. Bob taught me so much, most of all, how the unexpected can happen through simple belief. No greater writer than Archibald MacLeish came to Rhinelander one summer. A sophisticated guy. He could not believe the world he had entered. Imagine these students being exposed to this man who could not thank Robert E. Gard enough for putting *him* so close to the creative process. Long may the banner of SOA wave over the battlefields of ignorance!

I never asked for payment for teaching at the SOA, although I did ask that the school cover my expenses, which included travel as well as the rent for a cabin on a nearby lake. At the time, our family could not afford spending time at a lake cottage. While I taught at the school, Ruth and our three kids met new friends and had a great time in the water.

During the years I taught at SOA, I also began teaching weeklong writing workshops at The Clearing, located near Ellison Bay, Wisconsin. The school's founder, Danish-born landscape architect Jens Jensen, saw The Clearing as a place where people could renew their connection with nature. My first class was held in 1990, and I continued to teach there for nearly thirty years.

I wrote often in my journal about experiences at The Clearing. On October 11, 2011, I noted:

> Last Saturday was a beautiful fall day at The Clearing in Door County where thirty of us gathered for my annual one-day writing workshop that I call "Writing from Your Life." Plenty of fall color. The waters of Green Bay

Beginning in 1990 and for nearly thirty years I taught writing workshops at The Clearing in Door County.

were deep slate; the birch still showed some yellow and the sky was clear and blue.

The writers gathered to share stories—stories of early memories, of first toys, of growing up, of first jobs for pay, of joyous moments and many not as joyous as a few tears fell.

These writers of several generations filled pages with tales from their lives—stories long forgotten, by some at least. They shared their tales with each other and laughed and nodded knowingly, for though the details may have been different, the stories of each generation had many similarities as well.

Why do it? Why spend a gorgeous late autumn day writing stories? Because we are each a story, more accurately we are each a collection of little stories contributing to a larger one. Our stories make us human. When we forget our stories, we forget who we are.

From 2001 to 2006, I also taught a weeklong Write from Your Life workshop for the Write by the Lake program of UW–Madison Continuing Studies. The Write by the Lake program developed a national reputation, attracting students from near and far. Unfortunately, because of budget challenges, the UW discontinued the program in 2021.

In addition to formal writing programs, over the years I have taught daylong and shorter writing workshops at several public libraries and at Loras College in Iowa; the Monroe Arts Center in Monroe, Wisconsin; the Green Lake Writer's Institute in Green Lake; and the Edgerton Book Festival. I enjoy interacting with students, and I am pleased to be able to help them write their memoirs, whether they plan to share them with families and friends or seek publication.

ADVICE TO MY YOUNGER SELF

Someone recently asked me, "If you could go back and talk to your beginning self as a writer, what would you share based on what you have learned over the more than fifty years that you have been writing?" Here is my response.

- Keep a journal.
- Develop the discipline to keep writing even when the rejections are many and the road ahead is strewn with rocks and mudholes.
- Allow your creative self to come forward. It is there, but sometimes it is shy and reluctant to come out of the shadows. Encourage it.
- Write simply.
- Appreciate the power of a good story.
- Develop basic skills: spelling, grammar, sentence structure, etc.
- Use all your senses when writing.
- Learn to be patient. Writing takes time. Revision takes time. Editors need time. Publishers need time.
- Realize that you will spend time marketing and promoting your writing. It is part of your responsibility as a writer.
- Research is important, whether it is for fiction or nonfiction writing. And double-check your sources.
- Keep a good record of the research you do, whether it is interview notes, a photocopy of some statistics, or notes from a reference book. Nothing is more frustrating than trying to find a piece of research for a footnote.

- Throw nothing away. Keep all rough drafts and rejected manuscripts. All illustrations. Someday they may become valuable.
- Don't be afraid to ask for help. With research. With editing and rewriting. With reactions to what you have written. You may have to pay for editorial help. It is worth it.
- Don't expect to get rich.
- Don't be too hard on yourself.
- Enjoy the journey.

20 Columns, Blogs, and Online Writing

When I stopped writing columns for the *Waushara Argus* in 1976, I had no intention of picking it up again. Then in January 2013, Jim Massey, editor of the farm weekly *The Country Today*, asked if I would be interested in writing a weekly column about life on the farm for his newspaper. I said I would have to think about it. It had been many years since I had written newspaper columns. Jim then said, "I'll pay you top dollar."

I agreed to write two articles a month for a column titled Stories from the Land and did so through December 2019. I checked Jim's "top dollar" and learned that, considering inflation, I was earning the same for the *Country Today* column as I had received for the *Waushara Argus* columns I began writing in 1966. But I soon discovered that the benefits of column writing go far beyond the money. Not long after my column began running, emails from readers began arriving, and people attending my book talks mentioned my column as well. Many of my column readers said their growing-up years on a farm were similar to mine and thanked me for reminding them about those times.

In spring 2014, another opportunity to write a column arose. After I spoke at an annual meeting of the Richland Electric Cooperative, the co-op's manager, Shannon Clark, contacted me to ask if I would write a column for the group's monthly newsletter. The articles for this column, titled Rural Ramblings, were relatively short, five hundred to six hundred words, and appeared through December 2020. This one I wrote for the February 2020 newsletter:

SKUNK GREASE AND WHISKEY SLINGS

Often when I am talking to groups about what it was like on the farm back in the 1930s and 1940s, this question comes up, "What did you do when you got a cold?" As anyone knows who lived on a farm during those couple of decades, you never saw a doctor unless you were near death. The idea of going to a doctor with a cold, no matter how bad, was just not done.

What was done? A teakettle stood on the back of our wood burning kitchen stove, a bit of steam trickling from its spout. The teakettle was our sole source of hot water, as we had no indoor plumbing and I had never heard of such a thing as a water heater. Upon noticing that one of my brothers or I was coming down with a cold, before going to bed, my mother poured some hot water from the teakettle into a glass. She let it cool a bit and then added a jigger of "medicinal" whiskey, kept on the shelf for just this, and only this purpose. She also added a little honey. "Drink this," my mother would say. It was the most awful thing I had ever tasted—and to this day I cannot stand the smell or the taste of whiskey. She called the concoction a "whiskey sling."

On my chest she would rub not VapoRub, which I suspect they couldn't afford, but—don't fall over now—skunk grease. My Uncle Fred, a farmer but also a trapper, regularly trapped among other critters in the wild, skunks. He would render the grease from them, and give my dad a small jar of this "special" grease as my dad sometimes called it. By the way, skunk grease has no smell at all.

My mother would rub an ample amount of skunk grease on my chest, and then cover it with a piece of red flannel. Still wearing my long underwear, which I did both day and night, she would paddle me off to bed. As for many others who grew up on farms during the time when I did, woodstoves provided the heat for the house. My brothers and I shared a bedroom through which the stove pipe from the dining room heater passed. The stove pipe was supposed to keep the bedroom warm, which it did when the stove was going. But usually around midnight, the stove would sputter out, and a great chill came over our old farm house, especially our upstairs bedroom.

With a whiskey sling on the inside and healthy dose of skunk's grease on the outside, I crawled under a pile of covers that allowed no movement once all the quilts and blankets were in place. After a few minutes I would begin to sweat, and sweat all night I did. Usually, not always, by the next day I was considerably better, at least I said I was because I didn't look forward to another evening treatment of skunk's grease and a whiskey sling.

In March 2018, Colleen Kottke, the editor of the *Wisconsin State Farmer*, contacted me. "We'd like to run your blog as a weekly column," she said. I had begun writing a blog in 2007 that I share with readers on my website and on my Facebook page. (The term *blog* is short for "web log" and refers to a sort of online journal.) Publishing my blog as a column in the *Wisconsin State Farmer*, where it is titled Sit Awhile, increased its readership several times over. From 2019 to 2021, I also wrote two articles a month on Wisconsin agriculture history for a column in *Agri-View*, a weekly agriculture newspaper.

I continue to write stand-alone articles, though not as many as I did when I began freelance writing. Occasionally one of my writing students asks, "What's the difference between a column and an article?" A simple distinction is that a column usually appears regularly under the same title; articles usually run once. In addition, a column is often shorter than an article. My columns range between 250 and 800 words; articles I write are usually 1,500 words or longer. Articles typically are unbiased, while in columns I am free to express my opinions. I do avoid sharing anything about politics, religion, or relatives. I want a broad sweep of people to enjoy my writing, not only those who agree with me.

When I began a full-time writing career, the internet was not yet in widespread use. Today the internet offers many opportunities for writers. With the help of my nephew Matt Apps, I created a website for my writing work in October 2001. It was Matt who steered me toward writing my weekly blog. I began writing it in 2007 and continue to write it today. At the time of this writing, I have written 764 weekly blog entries. Unlike almost all of my other published writing, my blog posts are unedited, except by Ruth and me. There is no rejection, and every blog appears—the good, the bad, and the ugly. Here is the first blog that I wrote, on March 8, 2007:

LIVING A COUNTRY YEAR

I've tried something new with my upcoming book, *Living a Country Year* (Voyageur Press) which comes out in late May this year. I've combined story-telling with several what I call witticisms and advice—for each month of the year. Then, by digging into my grandmother's and my mother's old recipe boxes, I've added an appropriate recipe here and there. For instance, for March, I wrote:

· When you begin too much, you accomplish little.

· I met a fellow the other day who talked nonstop and didn't say a thing.

· It's okay to not know and admit it. Not knowing is the beginning of great wisdom.

I began including "The Old Timer Says" sayings that summer. Here is the first: "Life is like a river. There are twists and turns, quiet spots and rapids, deep pools and shallow flats. But a river is always moving. Always the same but always different."

Each blog usually includes a 250-word story or essay, an "Old Timer Says" statement, a list of upcoming events where I am speaking, and instructions for where to buy my books.

I wrote the following blog post in May 2020, when the COVID-19 epidemic closed schools and businesses and travel was discouraged.

THE IMPORTANCE OF HUMOR
May 15, 2020

During these difficult times, I remember the humor and laughter on the farm when I was a kid. Humor was a way of making a bad situation better, of finding something good in something that was awful. Of evoking laughter in a situation that was often filled with tears. Stories about a farmstead fire, a charging mad bull, or a tipped over pickup truck. Stories about minor and sometimes not so minor injuries caused by poor judgment or lack of knowledge.

Rural humor included practical jokes ranging from smearing Limburger cheese on the muffler of a newly-weds' car, to stuffing rocks in a grain sack so that the fellow carrying the grain from the threshing machine to granary walked with a staggering gait and a look that said, "I've never carried such heavy grain."

Humor allowed country people to live through the tough times, when the rains didn't come and the crops dried up, when a friend or relative died, when milk prices fell, when someone in the family was injured. Country humor was homemade; it was of the people. It was humor that came from the land. And although it may have evoked a belly laugh or sometimes only a chuckle, it cheered people up. For country people, good weather nourished their crops; humor nourished their souls.

I'm reminded of the story about the fellow driving along who spotted a sign that read: "Boat for sale." Behind the sign was a lawn mower and a wheelbarrow. The fellow stopped, interested in buying a boat. "Saw your sign," the fellow said, "but all I see is a wheelbarrow and a lawnmower."

"Yup," the man standing by the sign said, "And they're boat for sale."

THE OLD TIMER SAYS: A good laugh is often the best medicine.

Over time, "The Old Timer Says" began to take on a life of its own. A couple years ago, Kate Thompson, my editor at the Wisconsin Historical Society Press, asked if I would be interested in publishing a writer's journal, in which I would include a brief introduction to journaling, why it is important, and some tips for keeping a journal, followed by a series of blank pages for writing. Scattered throughout the book, released in 2020, are Old Timer sayings as prompts for writing.

In 2009, Matt set me up on Facebook. I began posting my blog on my Facebook page every week and immediately increased the readership of my blog by several times. For several months in 2020, I posted an "Old Timer Says" statement on my Facebook page. It was fun to watch the number of "likes" I received for each entry and read people's comments. For example, during the first week in August 2020, I posted this saying: "When you are doing nothing, how do you know when you are finished?" Within twenty-four hours I had 110 likes and a variety of comments: "That's the beauty of it, it never is done," "I feel I do nothing well," "When everything has been said and done, there is nothing more to say or do," and several more. Other popular Old Timer Says posts have been "There is great beauty in silence," with comments such as "So very true," and "That is why silence is golden," and "A good night's sleep can do much to calm an angry mind," with a favorite comment: "Naps help, too."

21   Book Talks

While the internet has made it possible for authors to do promotional work on their own, book marketing is still a responsibility shared by publisher and author. It's a lot of work and takes loads of time, but I have enjoyed the challenge of developing new ways to sell my books.

Early on, I discovered the importance of making personal appearances to promote my books. A book talk generates both publicity (media notices about the event always mention the book) and sales (either the hosting organization or the author sells books at the event). At one time, I was giving on average two talks a week during all but the winter months. Ruth traveled with me for many years, selling books before and after my talks. She knew the content of my books as well as I did and was an excellent salesperson.

I have given talks at a variety of places and for groups large and small: public libraries, bookstores, local historical societies, Rotary Club lunches, retired teacher groups, the Farm Toy Collectors' convention in Iowa, the Winchester Academy in Waupaca, as well as several conferences and conventions, including the Heartland Fall Forum hosted by the Midwest Booksellers Association

At the annual gathering of Midwest bookstores called Heartland Fall Forum, I spent time in my publishers' booths to meet booksellers and sign my books. In this photo from the 2015 show, I'm accompanied by Kathy Borkowski, Kate Thompson, Kristin Gilpatrick, and Halley Pucker, all with the Wisconsin Historical Society Press.

(formerly Upper Midwest Booksellers Association) and the annual conferences of the Wisconsin Library Association and American Library Association.

For several years, I gave talks at an Elderhostel program for retired adults held at the Green Lake Conference Center near Green Lake, Wisconsin. On October 5, 1999, I wrote in my journal:

> I have two Elderhostel sections meeting together each morning from 8:30 a.m. to 10 a.m.—a total of 75 people. The original group included 50 people. The second group of 25 had signed up to play golf, but the national Elderhostel office said they needed to also include some "edu-

cation" in their attendance plan. So, I have them in my group as well. I suspect they were not too happy pulled away from their first choice (golf) to become a part of a Wisconsin history group. I am here all week and will do a book a day: *Barns of Wisconsin, Cheese: the Making of a Wisconsin Tradition, One-Room Country Schools, Rural Wisdom,* and *When Chores Were Done.*

At the end of the week, I was very tired and not sure I wanted to do this another year, if I was asked. I was cheered up, when after the last session, I got a standing ovation. The bookstore at the conference center also shared with me that "book sales were good."

Often the biggest and most important book talk of all is the book launch. The book launch introduces a new book to the public, with a flourish of advertising and promotion and a big crowd for the in-person event. For many years, I launched my new books at the Barnes & Noble at a mall in Madison. One of the first was in 1998, when Amherst Press published the first edition of *Cheese: The Making of a Wisconsin Tradition.* In researching the book, I had interviewed several cheese makers, both active and retired. Amherst invited them to the launch. Now about twenty-five cheese experts sat in the front row, with another one hundred or so cheese lovers behind them, all looking at me. My always-worry-too-much self wondered if they were there to check up on my facts. But at the end of my presentation, audience members lined up to buy the book, including the cheese makers. One retired cheese maker bought seven copies. "I want my grandchildren to know what I did," he said, smiling. I knew I had passed the test with the cheese makers.

In 2002, Amherst Press launched my two children's picture books, *Eat Rutabagas* and *Stormy*, at Barnes & Noble. Two weeks before the event, Ruth addressed about 150 personal invitations and we mailed them to my growing list of friends, past book buyers, former students, and others. Barnes & Noble provided the postage and advertised the event in its newsletter:

TUESDAY, AUGUST 6, 7:00 P.M.
New Children's Series by Jerry Apps

Storyteller, historian and best-selling author Jerry Apps warmed our hearts with his Rural Life series of books including *Rural Wisdom* and *When Chores Were Done*. Tonight, Apps will read from *Eat Rutabagas* and *Stormy*, which bring stories of living in the country to life for kids. Artist Annika Beatty-Andersen beautifully illustrated both books.

About sixty people attended the event, and I signed books for an hour. After the event, B&N's community relations manager, Sherry Klinkner, reported twenty-eight copies of *Rutabagas* and thirty-two copies of *Stormy* sold, along with a stack of my backlist titles. Not a bad night.

Today my publishers use social media to promote my events, and I do as well. I post launches and other appearances on my blog and Facebook. And whereas in the early years of my career I usually simply prepared notes for myself, today I often spend a fair amount of time creating a PowerPoint presentation and include photos from the book.

I have learned a few things about book launches:

- Check for competing events before selecting a date and time. In Wisconsin, especially avoid Green Bay Packers game days.

- Publicity prior to the event—sending a press release that leads to notices in local newspapers, appearing on the local TV "Live at 5" sorts of shows, etc.—is essential.

- Personal invitations via email increase attendance.

- Arrive at the event a half hour early. Check to see if the microphone is working. If using PowerPoint, check to see if the computer projector is working properly.

- Simple refreshments get people to stick around after the talk. Ruth often baked cookies; sometimes the bookstore or library provided refreshments.

- Provide the host a copy of the introduction you would like them to read about you before your talk.

- Standing at a podium gives you a place to set your notes and a copy of your book.

- Begin with a brief "why I wrote the book" to help personalize the conversation.

- Reading some brief passages from the book allows people to experience your writing style.

- A good talk usually lasts thirty to forty minutes, with ten to fifteen minutes for questions at the end. Any longer exceeds people's attention spans.

· Making yourself available to the audience is
part of the point of a book launch. I sign books
and chat with people as long as it takes, until
we are up against closing time for the venue.
I offer to sign backlist titles.

· After the event, it's good practice to send a
thank-you note to the person in charge of the
book launch.

Book festivals are another good place to market
books. Festivals feature a slate of authors who give talks
and sign books. Over the years I have spoken many times
at Wisconsin book festivals, including the Southeastern
Wisconsin Festival of Books, Edgerton Book Festival,
Wisconsin Book Festival, Fox Cities Book Festival, and
Central Wisconsin Book Festival.

I have also appeared at many bookstores to promote
both new releases and older titles. These stores come in
all sizes, from the little community book shops to the giant chains such as Barnes & Noble. Bookstores do a good
job promoting their events to bring in audience members, and they provide the added benefit of catching the
attention of customers who happen to be in the store and
may not be familiar with the featured book or author. For
this reason, signing books at a bookstore can be a hum-
bling experience. Once when I was signing at an independent bookstore, I asked a passerby who had stopped
at the table if she had heard of my book. "Can't say that I
have," the lady said. "What's it about?"

I told her about my new novel, *Tamarack River Ghost*.
"Oh," she said, interrupting me, "I'm really not very interested in that sort of thing." She walked away.

For many years, the first Saturday in December meant a trip to West Bend and a presentation at Fireside Books. Here is what I wrote in my journal after a 2011 visit:

Visiting an independent bookstore is like going home. The clerks greet you by name; they stand ready to help you find a particular book of interest; they chat with you about books they like and have recently read; and they ask you how things are going in your life. Sometimes, they even offer you a cup of coffee.

Fireside Books & Gifts in West Bend is such a store. I was there this past Saturday, when the weather was wet and cold, and the day more than a little dreary. I was giving a talk and signing books. Ruth was along, and as I signed books, she browsed and sought out Christmas presents.

This was my 12th consecutive year at the store, and what a pleasure it was. Dennis Uhlig, bookseller and event organizer extraordinaire, asked people to reserve seats ahead of time for my presentation—and they did. Dennis also made cookies for the crowd, following the recipe in one of my books.

The chairs were filled with more folks standing in the back—thanks to Dennis's promotional efforts. We stuck around until two-thirty, talking with people, talking about books—and chatting about how important it was to have a bookstore such as Fireside in their community. I signed a goodly number of books.

Unfortunately, Fireside Books is now closed. It is missed by many.

Gift shops have also invited me to speak and sell books. For many years I have signed books at Dregne's,

Sue and I signed copies of our *Old Farm Country Cookbook* at Dregne's in Westby in 2017.

a Scandinavian-themed gift shop in Ruth's hometown of Westby, Wisconsin, often during the weekend of Syttende Mai (May 17), Norwegian Independence Day. I also usually sign in the fall, on the store's anniversary. During these special events, the store attracts an enormous crowd from around the region and beyond. Here is what I wrote about my visit to the store in 2015:

> This past Saturday, Ruth and I helped Dregne's cele-
> brate 40 years on Westby's Main Street. When Dave and
> Jana Dregne bought the corner building in 1975, it was
> a full-service hardware store with nuts and bolts, and
> ropes and wrenches and all the rest that makes up a
> hardware store.
>
> But now, 40 years later, it's a gift shop worthy of a
> destination visit. Not just a gift shop either, but a Scan-
> dinavian gift shop that shines a bright light on Westby's
> Norwegian heritage. If you want authentic Norwegian
> sweaters and a lefse grill or maybe some Swedish clogs

and pair of Scandinavian mittens, this is the place. And much, much more of course.

An enormous crowd trailed through the store on Saturday, coming from near and far. A bus load of Norwegians, on tour from Norway, arrived, 40 of them, each one with a camera and a smile. I spent 15 minutes talking with a fellow from Oslo about Wisconsin's barns and silos, and comparing pictures in my book *Barns of Wisconsin* with Norwegian barns that he knew.

Dregne's also has a wide selection of books by local authors, and not so local—I was there signing books, sharing a table with Tomah author Larry Scheckel. It was a busy, interesting day. I signed a bunch of books as well.

Libraries are another important place to connect with readers. I have spoken at public libraries in every corner of Wisconsin, from south to north, east to west. One of my favorites is the Patterson Memorial Library in my hometown. In November 2016, I wrote in my journal:

What a rare treat it was on a sunny November Saturday morning when I parked my truck in front of the Patterson Memorial Library in Wild Rose. Steve, who was with me, heard the geese first and when we looked up to see a huge flock, more than one hundred I would estimate, winging over the library, and then proceeding to land on the millpond. The sycamore tree was dropping its enormous yellowish-brown leaves on the walkway to the library, and the rose bushes were still in bloom on this weekend morning in early November.

Steve and I were at the library to discuss our new book, *Roshara Journal*, a book about our Wild Rose

farm, which we have now owned for 50 years. A book
that included journal entries that I made when we first
acquired the place and continued to write as the years
passed. A book that is filled with Steve's four-color
photos, taken in all seasons of the year, telling the story
of the farm, in photographs.

Some 40 people turned out, many of them old
friends, my brother Darrel and his wife, Marilyn, my
brother Donald and his wife, Marcie, some cousins, and
even one or two who attended Wild Rose High School
when I was there many years ago. I have spoken many
times at the Patterson, Kent Barnard its able director.

For the past fifteen years, my central Wisconsin book
launch has been at the Patterson. In addition to helping
launch my new books, the Friends of the Patterson Library sell my books as a fundraiser for the library.

I've kept a tally of how many different Wisconsin
libraries I've spoken at, and in 2016, I appeared at my
125th, the Rock Springs Public Library. As Kristin Gilpatrick, sales and marketing manager for the Wisconsin
Historical Society Press, remembered, "We managed to
sneak in staff and cake to surprise you and treat the audience. Your off-the-cuff remarks about the importance of
libraries to authors and to reading were fantastic icing
on the cake!"

Not long ago, the word was that all public libraries
would close—the internet provides everything people
need to know, and libraries will join livery stables, ice
boxes, and buggy whips as artifacts of history. But as
Mark Twain once said, "The reports of my death have
been greatly exaggerated." This is certainly true of libraries, which are alive and well and booming in popularity.

The Wisconsin Historical Society Press provided a cake to honor the occasion of my appearance at my 125th library.

Of course, like all of our public institutions, our libraries need our continued support. Communities love their libraries—and depend on them.

I have spoken at many local historical societies and museums as well, from Platteville to Portage and from Stanley to New Lebanon. I had the privilege of contributing for twenty years to the Sheboygan County Research Center's Second Saturdays program. I remember the blustery fall day when I was scheduled to talk about *Barns of Wisconsin*. The program was new, and it was an experiment—who would turn out to hear some guy from Madison talk about barns? But the room was full (coffee and doughnuts certainly helped to swell the crowd). Ruth heard a couple of farmers talking: "Too wet to work in the fields today, anyway," one said, "so I thought I'd come and hear something about barns—and drink some coffee."

For many years I attended the trade show of the Midwest Independent Booksellers Association, a trade group for book retailers. The show has most often been held in Minneapolis. One of the most memorable was the first I attended, in 1982, the year the University of Wisconsin Press published *Breweries of Wisconsin*. While I signed free copies of the book, the press staff worked to take orders from the booksellers, distributors, publishers, and other members of the organization.

Before the show, UW Press staff had discussed novel ways to attract people to my *Breweries of Wisconsin* book signing. They landed on the idea of offering a small glass of free beer to everyone who visited the booth during the signing time. At the time, University of Wisconsin rules did not allow such a thing, but somehow the press marketing department convinced the powers that be that it was acceptable since they were not *selling* the beer. The line waiting for me to sign books was one of the longest I had ever seen, and I signed a pile of books that day.

I've had successful book events at a number of unusual venues. For several years, I have participated in a December holiday event at McFarlanes' Hardware in Sauk City. You might not think of a hardware store as a place for author book presentations and signings. But McFarlanes' does it well. The presentation is often broadcast live by a local radio station. I wrote this in my journal after a McFarlanes' event in 2017:

> It had snowed enough to remind us that winter was just around the corner. And if the snow wasn't enough, a cold northwest wind put an exclamation point on that reality. Sue and I were on our way to Sauk City, to McFarlanes'. To a hardware store that sells more than

nuts and bolts, and paint and wrenches. McFarlanes' also sells books.

Starting at ten a.m., Sue and I were a part of an hour-long, live radio broadcast originating at the hardware store and aired on Baraboo's 99.7 FM and 740 AM radio stations. Rauel LaBreche, animated and with never a dull word, hosted the show, asking us questions: "What makes *Old Farm Country Cookbook* different from other cookbooks, why did Sue refuse to try the fried squirrel recipe, why did I write the *Never Curse the Rain* book," and more.

Some 40 plus people were seated in the little studio, carved out of a corner of the hardware store, listening, laughing—having a good time. Sandwiched in between the questions and answers, Curt Meine and his Prairie Spies musical group offered live holiday music. Curt, beyond his musical skills, is also a well-known author and Aldo Leopold's biographer. Sue and I had a fun time, and we signed a bunch of books as well.

One of the most important lessons I've learned about promoting my books is to meet people wherever they are: in their communities and where they are comfortable. Not everyone visits bookstores or libraries or literary festivals. For ten years, Ruth and I attended the annual farm toy show in Iowa. I wrote this in my journal after one of those visits:

They came from throughout the country, from Canada and several other countries. They gathered at Dyersville, Iowa, a little town west of Dubuque. Farmers mostly, those who still worked the land, and those who were retired but knew the stories of farming and farm

10th Annual
2011

FROM THE LAND

A Gathering of Traditional Crafts and
Skills With Demonstrations

October 22-23

Saturday 10-4 & Sunday 10-3

On the Toll/Londowski Family Farm
One mile west of the
Hwy. 49/Co. Rd. J intersection

Green Lake, WI

*Knowledge and techniques given from the
heart by people who truly enjoy what they do.*

Baskets • Bead Art • Whimsy • Folk Art Painting
Wood Carving • Pottery • Rugs & Weaving
Handmade Soaps • Jewelry & Clothing • Wood
Furniture • Papiér Maché • Metal Sculptures
Photography • Pine Needle Art • Candles
Pumpkins • Gourds • Apples • Honey • Kettle Corn
Pasture-fed Beef • Chicken • Lamb • Pork
Smoked Meat • European Bakery
Plenty of parking in west adjacent field

Speaker: SATURDAY ONLY - Jerry Apps
11:00 a.m. "Horse Drawn Days"
1:00 p.m. "Lighter Side of Country Life"
Music:
Folksinger & Songwriter Jim Anger both days
Antique Tractor Show Both Days

Over the years, I have spoken at nearly every sort of venue there is,
from festivals to saloons. I remember speaking in the empty hay
loft of an old barn near Dodgeville. Close to a hundred people had
gathered there, and the owner feared the barn would collapse with all
the weight. It didn't.

life. Often three generations together, grandparents, mom and dad, and the grandkids. Looking at toy tractors and swapping "I remember when" stories. So many stories, nonstop stories from Friday evening until Sunday afternoon.

I sat behind a table piled high with my books as folks stopped by to chat. Their caps identified them—John Deere, Allis Chalmers, International Harvester, Oliver. Their caps told me which tractor was their choice and the source of their stories. Their sweat shirts carried on their infatuation with a certain kind of tractor: "Real friends don't allow their friends to drive red tractors." (A John Deere tractor lover for those who don't know about the friendly competition between red (International) and green (John Deere) tractors.)

One little boy—lots of kids of all sizes and ages attended—wore a shirt with the words "I was born in a barn" plastered across the front. "Were you really born in a barn?" I asked.

"I don't know," he said smiling. His mother was smiling, too.

Other sweatshirt messages: "Real men use duct tape," "My tractor's my first love," and "Still plays with tractors."

A cute little boy's sweatshirt said: "Dirt Rocks." Another little boy's shirt: "I move dirt."

Some 10,000 plus folks attended the event—most of them walked by my table at one time or another. I signed a goodly number of books. And had great fun swapping old timer farmer stories.

For several years I was invited to speak at Farm Technology Days, an outdoor educational event sponsored by

the UW College of Agricultural and Life Sciences in cooperation with a local county extension office and many
local farmers, associations, and business volunteers.
There I met many people who shared an interest in the
topics I write about. Here is what I wrote after the 2015
event, held near Sun Prairie:

> Last Tuesday I spoke at Farm Technology Days; it was
> on the 6,000-acre Statz Brothers' farm near Sun Prairie
> in Dane County. The event drew some 45,000 people
> over the three-day run. The weather was cool and dry,
> perfect for an outdoor event where people could see
> the present and the future for agriculture. From buzz-
> ing drones, to the biggest tractors I've ever seen, from
> demonstrations on harvesting alfalfa to viewing the
> most up-to-date technology for milking cows. It was
> all there.
>
> I spoke on Tuesday morning, and talked about
> the past, when we farmed 160 acres without electric-
> ity, milked a small herd of cows by hand, cut hay with
> horses, and communicated with a party-line telephone.
> And a drone was a male honey bee. I reminded the es-
> timated 150 people in my audience that to know where
> we are going, whether it is in farming or in life, we must
> know where we've been. I emphasized the importance
> of knowing our histories.

22 Stories from the Road

One of the benefits of being a published writer has been the opportunity to travel the state extensively. Some years were busier than others, especially during the years that I was writing full-time: I traveled 13,370 miles in 2007; 13,172 in 2008; 11,298 in 2012. In recent years, the Wisconsin Historical Society Press has helped with the driving and bookselling. After spending so many years on the road, Ruth and I have many stories to tell.

I remember well the first book signing that I did. It was in 1970, shortly after the publication of *The Land Still Lives*. I was at a little bookstore in Madison, feeling a bit nervous because I had never done this before. What should I expect at a book signing? I had seen authors in TV shows with a big pile of books on a table and long lines of people waiting to get their books signed. But that is not what happened at my first book signing. First, the stack of books was not a tall one—there were maybe a half dozen or so. And the long line of fans was nonexistent. For a considerable time, the line numbered zero. Then a well-dressed middle-aged woman stopped at my table. I greeted her.

Connecting with people while out on the road makes all the challenges of travel worthwhile.

"Is this your book?" she asked as she picked up a copy. "What are you asking for it?"

"It sells for $5.95," I said, smiling.

"$5.95!" she said, raising her voice. "That's outrageous. $5.95 for a book," she huffed. "Nobody pays that kind of money for a book." She slammed down the book and stalked off.

I don't recall how many books I signed that day, probably three or four. Nearly fifty years later, the book was published as an anniversary edition. The price: twenty-five dollars. So far, I haven't heard anyone complain about the price.

Interestingly, the most challenging part of many trips has been finding the place where I'm supposed to speak. Once I was scheduled to speak at a fairgrounds in southwestern Wisconsin. When I asked my host the location of the fairgrounds, he answered, "Oh, everybody knows where the fairgrounds is." Everybody but me. I had to stop at a local gas station to get the directions.

When GPS technology became available, finding places became easier—but the GPS didn't always have the right answer. One time when I was following my new GPS's directions to Monroe High School, I found myself at the entrance to the local landfill. As Halley Pucker, one of my early Wisconsin Historical Society Press drivers, later said, "It was funny how the GPS *always* had us take the backroads and country roads." I suspect the GPS was providing the shortest route, even if it took us down seldom-traveled, narrow, and crooked country roads. But by and large, GPS was a vast improvement over relying on a paper map, plus it informed us how long the drive would take, something that had always been a bit of a mystery.

Weather has sometimes been a challenge as much as following directions was. Jen Rubin, another WHS Press staffer, commented, "Once when driving home from a small-town library during a whiteout snowstorm, I remember thinking, we did not sell nearly enough books for me to die driving Jerry Apps back home!"

Chris Caldwell, WHS Press events coordinator and my most recent driver, recounted a night I was speaking at Belleville High School. Storm clouds were building in the west. Chris said, "I remember getting lost on the way back (a frequent leitmotif in the saga of our travels) and the skies opening up—torrential downpour. I think we ended up in Brooklyn, Wisconsin, before we whipped out the map and I got my bearings back. Flash flood–like conditions all the way home. When I parked my car in the lot outside my apartment the water was ankle deep."

Chris also reminded me that the weather was notable for an event in Darlington for my book *Never Curse the Rain*: "Heavy rains and flooding in the preceding week had washed out the bridge over the Pecatonica River. If any group had a reason to curse the rain . . . One audience member told me that because he lived just on the other side of the bridge from the library, he had to drive forty-five minutes out of his way to get there." Despite the obstacles, a hundred people attended.

When we visited far-flung places, we would often stay for the night. The lodging stories never end. I've stayed in motel rooms that ranged from extraordinarily nice to one so small you had to back into the bathroom— well, maybe not quite that bad. I remember one time when I was to speak at Stonefield Historic Site and had reservations at a Cassville motel. I didn't arrive until a few minutes after 6 p.m. "Oh," the desk clerk said when I wanted to check in. "We didn't think you were coming, so we gave your room to another guest. Sorry."

One of the most unusual places Ruth and I stayed was a bed-and-breakfast near Clear Lake that was designed to replicate the set of the famed *Andy Griffith Show* that ran on TV from 1960 to 1968. The owners belonged to an Andy Griffith Show fan club. Another bed-and-breakfast, this one in Sheboygan Falls, was a nice place— except that the owner forgot to make us breakfast.

Kristin Gilpatrick, who besides being the sales and marketing manager for the Wisconsin Historical Society Press is also frequently one of my drivers, tells a great story about our hotel adventures in Eau Claire:

> Of all the memories, all the trips, all the chats, and all the miles, there is one event that rises—maybe sinks—above

all others. On May 11, 2015, I picked you up to speak at the Wisconsin History Tour's Writers' Forum with Michael Perry and John Hildebrand in Eau Claire. It had been difficult finding a hotel in Eau Claire that would honor the state rate that state employees/guests are allowed to pay (seventy dollars at the time, as I recall). I finally found a recognizable chain hotel at the northernmost exit of Eau Claire and made the reservation.

We left late afternoon, arriving just around 8 p.m. I had to drop off materials for the morning, so I dropped you off at the hotel in the dark—located on the north side of town and surrounded by truck stops, definitely not the tourist area. As we pulled in, you were thinking you could walk next door to what looked like a bar with maybe a little grill for a late dinner. Upon closer inspection, you realized it was in fact a strip club with more on the menu than someone on the state agency dime should be ordering. There was a McDonald's across the busy eight-lane highway from the hotel, but with cane in hand you didn't feel lucky enough to test your Frogger-playing skills in real life. So, you stayed in, figuring you would grab something from the vending machine.

Seizing a plastic bowl of Ramen noodles to make in your room, you inquired at the front desk for a spoon. Since they offered "hot breakfast" in the morning, you figured that was a simple request. After much searching, it was discovered that all utensils were under lock and key and could not be available until morning.

While I was driving through a Burger King downtown, you were sitting on the edge of your bed, waiting for the Ramen noodles to soften in the in-room microwave. Only after you got up to retrieve "dinner" did you see the sign by the bathroom faucet that said:

"water not potable due to formaldehyde contamination. Do not drink or consume." You ate the Ramen noodles you prepared with that water anyway, sitting on the edge of the bed and balancing the noodles into your mouth with your pocket knife. The next day, when you filled me in, I expressed horror that this was your dinner, to which you replied, "It wasn't all bad. There were peas in the Ramen noodles. That was a nice surprise."

Sometime before I arrived back at the hotel, you had done some additional assessing of the situation and left the following voicemail on my hotel room phone. "Kristin, Jerry here. I've had a look around and I am pretty sure that you are the only woman in this hotel so be sure to double lock your door. Oh, and don't drink the water. See you in the lobby for breakfast!"

In the morning, you were up bright and early and already down in the lobby when I arrived. We both skipped the breakfast part as the smell of stale cigarettes sort of overpowered the eggs and biscuits. I first spotted you looking pensively out the big lobby window into the morning darkness. "Hi Jerry," I approached. "What are you thinking about?"

"The car fire in the parking lot," you replied bluntly. I was shocked, but sadly not surprised, when I looked out and saw the fire truck, cop car, and the burnt remains of some guest's car. Fortunately, the state van—just a few stalls away—was unharmed. I was relieved, mostly because I would not have wanted to do the paperwork that would have been required. To say we got out of there quickly would not accurately describe the speed of our exit from what is without a doubt the worst book event hotel experience I've ever had.

One of the more unusual happenings at a book signing occurred on a November Saturday at the Mall of America in Bloomington, Minnesota. I was signing books in a store called A Simpler Time. The mall was busy, and it was a good day. By 5:00 p.m. I had signed fifty books. Just as I was finishing signing, the mall lights blinked twice and went out, on all three floors. With only emergency lighting to see by and no power for the cash register, store manager Jeff King wrote out the last few charges in longhand. Ruth and I bid Jeff good-bye and headed back to Madison with another story to add to our collection.

Of course, one of the most pleasurable things about traveling the state (and beyond) is the many interesting people I meet. I remember signing books at a bookstore in Kenosha on a sunny fall Sunday in late October one year. Unfortunately, it was a Green Bay Packers Sunday, and there was almost nobody in the bookstore. After an hour had passed without my signing a single book, a young man arrived at my table with his daughter in tow. He said he was there to help his daughter buy her first book. The little girl, probably about three years old, began paging through several of my books with a serious look on her face. She would pick up one book, turn a few pages, and then put it back down. This went on for several minutes. Her father stood by quietly as the girl continued to inspect my book collection. Finally, she picked up a copy of *Stormy*, one of my children's picture books. "Daddy, I think I would like this one," she said. I proceeded to sign it, inscribing it to her. She was smiling as I wrote her name in the book. That was one of my best signing days, although I sold only a handful of books.

LIFE ON THE ROAD

Some aspiring writers don't realize how much effort it takes to promote and sell books. Below is a typical schedule of my speaking and book-signing engagements—this one from fall 2014—that will give you a hint of the work involved.

- October 17, 7:00 p.m. Park Falls Library, Park Falls. *Limping through Life*.
- October 20, Noon. Rib River Ballroom, Marathon City. German-American Group. *Limping through Life*.
- October 22, 3:00 p.m. Brillion Library. *Limping through Life*.
- October 23, 2:45–3:30 p.m. Wisconsin Library Association, Green Bay. *Letters from Hillside Farm*.
- October 26, 10:00 a.m.–2:00 p.m. Grafton Book Festival, Liberty Memorial Library, Grafton. *Limping through Life*.
- November 2, 9:00 a.m.–4:00 p.m. The Clearing, Door County. Writing from Your Life workshop.
- November 2, 4:00–6:00 p.m. Book signing. The Clearing, Door County.
- November 6, 3:30 p.m. UW PLATO group, Oakwood West, Madison. *The Quiet Season*.
- November 7, 7:00 p.m. Baraboo Public Library. *Ringlingville USA*.
- November 9, 9:30 a.m. Sheboygan County Research Center, Plymouth. *Limping through Life*.
- November 10: 3:30 p.m. Books and Company bookstore, Oconomowoc. *The Quiet Season*.

Kristin Gilpatrick remembered a conversation she heard when she drove me to the Tri-County Tractor Show in Plainfield, Wisconsin, where I spoke about *Limping through Life*. "Not one but two polio survivors and their families showed up to thank you for writing that book. They drove hours (one from Chicago) and trailed down that gravel road into the show grounds just to have the chance to thank you for bringing attention to their history and their story."

Chris Caldwell recalled a visit to Seymour to promote *Rural Wit and Wisdom*. He noted, "Seymour has a population of 3,451, and we got 225 of them into the basement of the Emmanuel Lutheran Church. A number of the attendees were residents of area memory care facilities, brought in to hear stories of the past that would resonate with them and help jog some of their own memories of growing up."

Speaking with people and signing books has been about so much more than selling copies. It is the many people I've met and their encouragement to "keep on writing" that make it truly rewarding.

23   Social Media and Other Internet Adventures

The website I set up in 2001 with the help of my nephew Matt is an important tool for connecting with current and potential readers. Matt continues as my webmaster, adding and updating content as needed. On the site (www.jerryapps.com), I share my blog posts, information about all my books, dates for workshops and book events, and ways of contacting me. The site also includes a link to my Facebook page.

I joined Facebook in 2009, and at this writing I have nearly five thousand "friends," the limit imposed by Facebook on personal accounts. I try to post to Facebook several times a week, including new book announcements and new reviews. I have now also used Facebook's broadcast feature, Facebook Live, many times to discuss my books live with viewers. People watching and listening can ask questions at the end of a presentation. In cooperation with the Wisconsin Historical Society Press, I have done several twenty- to thirty-minute live programs featuring one of my books. When schools closed due to the COVID-19 pandemic in 2020, the WHS Press quickly designed a series of weekly Storytime Live Facebook programs for kids learning virtually at home. We were all learning how to use this new form of communication when I made my first appearance for the series, reading and sharing pictures from my children's picture book *Eat Rutabagas*. The Press later shared the video on its YouTube channel, and several thousand people have now watched the show, both kids and adults. I did five more Storytime Lives, plus a twenty-minute talk on a Wednesday evening for the WHS Press series for adults called Book Bites.

When travel started to become difficult for me and I planned to cut back on in-person presentations, I tried Skype as an alternative. Skype is a way to connect from computer to computer in a video phone call. I discovered that people preferred to see me in person—and indeed for one event, not one person attended when they learned I was not going to be there in person. Then in 2020, as COVID-19 caused the cancellation of face-to-face meetings, Zoom quickly became more popular than Skype. Zoom is a web-based video tool that allows people to meet online, with or without video, from any location that has a computer and a Wi-Fi connection.

One of my first Zoom presentations was hosted by the Columbus (Wisconsin) Public Library. They had originally scheduled me for an in-person presentation, and when it had to be cancelled, they turned to Zoom. I promoted the event on my Facebook page, and people turned out from far beyond Columbus. We had a good crowd.

For most of my face-to-face presentations, I used a PowerPoint series of slides to illustrate my talk. Could PowerPoint be incorporated into a Zoom presentation?

My next attempt was at the virtual Central Wisconsin Book Festival. Chris Caldwell of the WHS Press and I did a trial run. The sound was garbled—it sounded like I was talking underwater—and the pictures were breaking up. We experimented with turning the video off when I was speaking. That helped but did not completely solve the problem. I went ahead with it, despite feeling it was not up to the standards I feel a professional presentation ought to reach.

Chris and I talked at length about how to make things better, as we had the Fox Cities Book Festival coming up. I replaced my old router with a new one. The Fox Cities Book Festival went on, and my presentation's technical quality was better, but still lacking. What to do?

I did some research and learned that if one's computer is hard-wired to Wi-Fi, the connection is stronger and more stable. I also learned that laptop computers do not have the highest-quality cameras, speakers, or microphones. Early in the summer of 2020, my desktop computer died. I bought a faster one with more storage capacity, plus a professional-grade microphone and a webcam, both of which I attached directly to my computer. So far, this new system seems to run with perfection—no glitches, no garbled or delayed sound.

I'm slowly learning this new approach to presenting, which allows me to stay at home but still be in contact with people interested in learning about my books. Besides avoiding hazardous winter roads, the advantages are many: there's usually no limit on audience size, and people can attend from any location with a Wi-Fi connection. The downsides: the learning curve can be steep, especially for this old-timer. Human error in using the

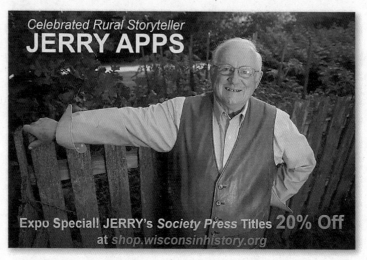

Celebrated Rural Storyteller
JERRY APPS

Expo Special! JERRY's *Society Press* Titles 20% Off
at shop.wisconsinhistory.org

Since 2020, I've talked about my books at the virtual version of PBS Wisconsin's Garden & Landscape Expo.

online system is always a possibility, and not all computers and Wi-Fi systems work equally well. I miss in-person interactions with audiences, reading their facial expressions and discerning whether what I'm saying is making sense, hitting an emotional button, or striking a funny bone. And of course, we're still figuring out how to sell books to audience members during a virtual event.

A number of the virtual events I've done since 2005 are now available for viewing on YouTube, including the five hour-long PBS Wisconsin documentaries, as well as several of the Facebook Live programs and recorded in-person presentations.

With the assistance of my daughter-in-law Natasha, I set up a second website solely for the purpose of offering an online book club. One of the first books I selected for the book club was *Limping through Life*. Here is how we promoted the club:

THE STORIES FROM THE LAND BOOK CLUB JULY 2020 SELECTION IS ...

Limping through Life: A Farm Boy's Polio Memoir

Purchase at your local bookstore, or online from Bookshop.org

In his most personal book, Jerry Apps, who contracted polio at age twelve, reveals how the disease affected him physically and emotionally, profoundly influencing his education, military service, and family life and setting him on the path to becoming a professional writer.

HOW TO PARTICIPATE IN THE BOOK CLUB

• Read the Book Club featured book.

• Think about and react to the prompt questions below from the author.

• Check back in regularly to see responses from other book club members and the author.

• Monitor the author's Facebook site for reminders about the Book Club. Visit www.facebook.com/jerryapps to follow the author on Facebook.

QUESTIONS:

1. Do you know anyone who had polio? What is their condition today? How have they coped as a polio survivor?

2. How would you compare the polio epidemic with the current COVID-19 pandemic?

3. Do you or do you know someone who remembers the polio epidemic (1945–1955)?

4. During the polio years many public events were cancelled and parks closed. How did people react?

5. What thoughts do you have about the treatment Jerry received?

6. What are your reactions as to how Jerry's father took over the physical therapy treatment by using a "farmer approach"?

7. What did you like about the book?

8. What didn't you like?

9. Any other thoughts you'd like to share?

Write your answers in the "Reply" space below. The book club will continue, starting July 1 for six weeks. Jerry will respond to your questions on Friday of each week.

The internet book club was moderately successful; about twenty people participated in the one I did on *Limping through Life*. My audience is a bit older, and they, like me, still prefer face-to-face contact.

The internet will be increasingly important in book promotions as we march into the future and as authors, publishers, and audience members become comfortable using it as a gathering space. One positive of the COVID-19 pandemic is that it forced many of us to become acquainted with new technology and new ways to get together and talk about books.

24 Radio and Television

Along with in-person book talks and signings, I have spent many hours appearing on radio and television programs to talk about my books. I got my first experience doing live radio shows in 1957, as part of my role as a University of Wisconsin extension agent in Green Lake County. After moving to Madison, I did radio shows related to my new books, the first one in 1970. And in the early 2000s, I did a number of three-minute taped radio shows for UW–Madison's Agricultural Journalism Department as part of a series called What's New in Agricultural and Life Science Research that aired on one hundred radio stations in the upper Midwest. For the What's New series, I included stories from several of my books about farm life when I was a kid. For example, on February 26, 2003, I taped eight shows, enough for two months, on country school winter games, blizzards, spring break-up, garden catalogs, and barns.

With years of networking, the backing of my publishers, and no small amount of persistence, I have landed many appearances on radio and television shows. I have appeared frequently with Pam Jahnke, whose *Midwest Farm Report* is broadcast on several radio stations and covers nearly all of Wisconsin. On the *Larry Meiller Show*, a fifty-year staple of Wisconsin Public Radio broadcast weekdays from 11:00 a.m. to 12:30 p.m., I have showcased many new books for Larry's vast audience across Wisconsin and beyond. Larry's fans call in to ask questions and offer their stories about the book or other topic being discussed.

My introduction to television appearances came in the early 1960s, when I worked as a university extension agent in Brown County and appeared on air with Orion Samuelson, then farm director for WBAY in Green Bay. I also did several programs for WMTV. Everything was live in those days; if you messed up, it was broadcast. I screwed up regularly, and those who watched my programs found great glee in reminding me of my screwups, but they kept watching nonetheless.

In my early years working at the university in Madison, I did little TV work, only an occasional short program on one of Madison's local stations talking about one

NEW BOOK: CIVILIAN CONSERVATION CORPS IN WISCONSIN

I've appeared frequently on local television stations, as in this interview with Madison News 3's Mark Koehn and Susan Siman for the release of *The Civilian Conservation Corps: Wisconsin's Nature Army at Work*.

of my books. After I moved from teaching to full-time writing, I began doing more TV appearances. In 1999, Wisconsin Public Television asked if I would help them produce a show on Wisconsin's old barns, featuring barn preservation work taking place around the state. I wrote much of the script and provided voice-over commentary. Here is what I wrote in my journal on January 7 of that year:

> A film crew from Wisconsin Public TV arrived yesterday to do another segment for a Barns program that they plan to air this summer. Elizabeth Koerner is the producer for the show. They filmed for about an hour. I talked about barn doors, weather vanes, cupolas, and mechanical hayforks. I'm anxious to see how it turned out.

My book *Cheese: The Making of a Wisconsin Tradition* had come out in 1998, and not long after I did the filming for the barn show, the Wisconsin Dairy Council asked if I'd be interested in doing publicity work promoting Wisconsin cheese in Illinois during National Dairy Month that June. It would include TV, radio, and newspaper interviews. On June 10, 1999, I wrote in my journal:

> I've just returned from a two-day trip to Illinois for the Dairy Council of Wisconsin. They are paying me $500.00 a day, plus expenses. I am pleased to promote Wisconsin cheese, and of course to promote my new book on that topic. So far, I have appeared on WREX-TV Rockford. I also did a half hour radio show with WROK-AM, an interview with the *Rockford Register Star*, a phone interview with the *Northwest Herald*, Crystal

Lake; and an interview with the Mid-West Dairymen's Cooperative. I did a radio interview with Orion Samuelson at the WGN studio in Chicago.

As I continued making appearances on local televisions stations, some bigger TV opportunities began arriving. While I was working on my book *Ringlingville USA*, I received a call from a film crew associated with the PBS program *History Detectives*. They were interested in filming early movie houses, and the Al. Ringling Theater in Baraboo was one of the candidates. On February 4, 2003, I spent four hours with a film crew at Circus World Museum, sharing history of the Ringling Brothers and Al Ringling's early contributions to the movie business. I was impressed with the size of the crew, which consisted of producer, director, actors, camera operators, sound technicians, and three assistants. The main actor, who was interviewing me as we walked across the Baraboo River, had a cold. Not far from her at all times was her assistant offering her toilet paper to blow her nose. As we walked across the bridge, she sniffled and the director shouted, "Cut." She blew her nose and we did it all over again—four times. We filmed until dark.

In 2007, I had an opportunity to talk about my cheese book on the History Channel. A TV crew from Los Angeles flew to Madison and interviewed several people, including me. I remember the interviewer asking me if I minded being called a "Cheesehead."

"Not at all," I replied, to her astonishment. For a few seconds she hesitated, not having gotten the answer she expected. Nevertheless, we chatted for nearly a half hour about cheese and Wisconsin.

In June of 2006, Carol Larson, a producer with Wisconsin Public Television (now PBS Wisconsin) contacted me and said WPT was interested in talking with me about future documentary productions. I wrote in my journal:

> I met with James Steinbach, WPT Director, Carol Larson, Producer, and Kathy Bissen, Program Director. We discussed their interest in doing a series of shows based on my farm related books beginning with *Old Farm*. They were also interested in doing a show on one-room schools, farming with horses, and Wisconsin's specialty crops such as mint, cucumbers, peas, ginseng and sphagnum moss. We'll see where all of this goes.

Three months later, I wrote this in my journal:

> I met Wednesday noon with Carol Larson and another producer from Wisconsin Public TV to discuss a show based on my upcoming book *Old Farm*. The second producer said the focus of the planned show was too narrow and the potential audience too limited. I don't know if this project is going anywhere.

In November, I wrote:

> I turned in the manuscript for *Old Farm* to Kate Thompson at the Wisconsin Historical Society Press today. I had lunch with Kate and Carol Larson from WPT to discuss a show related to the book. I learned that it would cost about $150,000 to produce the show, and most of the money has to be raised. Themes for the show might be the economic side of land restoration,

the history of the area, and what caring for the land was all about.

In March 2007, I wrote in my journal that filming of an *Old Farm* show was "stalled pending approval." On June 1, I noted, "WPT show appears to be a dead horse."

At that point I forgot about doing any documentaries with Wisconsin Public Television. But then, four years later, I spoke at a UW Alumni–Wisconsin meeting held at a resort north of Minocqua. My topic was Wisconsin's role in Prohibition, based on material I had written in my book *Breweries of Wisconsin*. This was just prior to the very popular PBS program on Prohibition developed by Ken Burns. At dinner that evening, I happened to sit next to James Steinbach, director of Wisconsin Public Television. As we chatted, Jim asked, without any prompting from me, "Say, Jerry, would you be interested in doing a documentary for us on what farm life was like when you were a kid?"

"Sure," I said, wondering if this would eventually find the same fate as the earlier conversations. But this time the situation was different. On October 25, 2011, I wrote in my journal:

I met with Mik Derks, producer for WPT, today. He shared that WPT is interested in doing an hour-long documentary with me sharing stories about my growing up years on a farm during the late 1930s and the 1940s. I couldn't believe it. I never did find out what discussions took place at WPT from four years ago when the possibility of a TV documentary was dead, to now, four years later when the interest appeared high.

A film crew appeared at my Waushara County farm on November 11, 2011. We were moving forward with the documentary. I wrote in my journal on that date:

An early snowstorm hit central Wisconsin today, causing the WPT film crew to drive three hours when it usually takes but two hours for the drive. They filmed for about an hour and a half, and then the power at the farm went out. They had no batteries, so no power, no filming. The crew packed up and drove back to Madison. I have heard nothing from the producer. Based on the short, interrupted interview, they may have given up on the idea.

What next? I wondered. I went back to my writing and doing various presentations and book signings around the state. But WPT was serious about the documentary. The film crew returned several times to the farm and also did considerable filming in and around Wild Rose. By October 2012, the documentary *Jerry Apps: A Farm Story* was complete. The show included several still photos contributed by people from the Wild Rose area: images of one-room country schools, making hay and threshing grain, cucumber picking, swimming at Little Silver Lake, and many others. The film also included several shots of Wild Rose's Main Street featuring the hardware store and the old Mercantile, still the largest building in the village, as well as the millpond and the old grist mill. The narration included stories from several of my books, including *Rural Wit and Wisdom, When Chores Were Done, Living a Country Year, Every Farm Tells a Story, One-Room Country Schools*, and *Old Farm: A History*.

The premier showing of the film was at the Wild Rose High School auditorium on October 15, 2012, at 5:30 p.m. The showing included a reception with light refreshments. There was no charge. Following the event, I wrote this in my journal:

> The first showing of *Jerry Apps: A Farm Story* last Monday evening at Wild Rose High School. More than 200 people attended. Positive reaction. The show is bringing back many memories. Future showing at Viroqua and Green Bay, before the show goes on the air November 28.

Jerry Apps: A Farm Story aired on all five Wisconsin Public TV stations on November 5, 2012, as part of WPT's pledge drive. The program was an hour long but was broken into segments, after which viewers were encouraged to pledge money to WPT. I was working live on the air during those pauses in the documentary to share background information about the show. Over the years I had done several TV shows, but never was I more anxious than I was on this night. Would the show be a complete flop? Would some of the early staff concerns about the "narrow" topic and few interested viewers prove true?

During this first pledge break, the phones began ringing and pledges began rolling in. Would this interest in the show continue as the showing progressed? It did. I was surprised. The Wisconsin Public TV people were surprised. In a December 10 email, Jon Miskowski from WPT reported, "*Farm Story* was the biggest show of the pledge drive, with *Downton Abbey* a strong second." The British series *Downton Abbey* was extremely popular in the United States at the time. Jon's final comment: "So you heard it here—Jerry Apps is bigger than *Downton Abbey*. That's saying a lot."

Wisconsin Public Television sold the airing rights for *Farm Story* to national PBS, and several PBS stations asked me to help with their pledge drives when they aired the program. I traveled to Minneapolis, Kansas City, Chicago, and Milwaukee to appear on behalf of those stations. All the travel reminded me of my years working for UW–Madison; I didn't especially care for it then, and now at sixty-nine years old, I cared for it even less. But once I arrived at each new station, I enjoyed meeting with and working with public television people and watching and learning how they did things. By August 2013, some sixty-five PBS stations in forty-nine states had aired *Farm Story*.

I began receiving emails and phone calls from people around the country who wanted to share their stories about growing up on a farm in Maine, North Carolina, Washington State, Pennsylvania. Although it took some time, I answered every email. My stories clearly had touched many people and had awakened memories of what life was like in rural areas, especially during the Great Depression and World War II. One evening the phone rang, and when I answered I heard, "Are you the fellow that writes those books about early life on the farm and did that TV show?"

"I am," I answered, wondering if I had said or written something he disagreed with or if he had found an error in one of my books. He told me his name and then for fifteen minutes proceeded to tell me nonstop about what farm life was like in Palmer, Alaska, where he lived and farmed. I had gotten him thinking, and remembering.

The premier showings of my PBS Wisconsin documentaries have brought out many people interested in sharing their own memories of country winters, attending a one-room school, and rural life in general.

PBS Wisconsin went on to produce four more hour-long documentaries, each based on one of my books: *A Farm Winter with Jerry Apps* (2013, based on *The Quiet Season*); *The Land with Jerry Apps* (2015, based on *Whispers and Shadows*); *Never Curse the Rain* (2017, based on the book *Never Curse the Rain*); and *One-Room School* (2018, based on the book *One-Room Country Schools*). Much to my surprise, *A Farm Winter with Jerry Apps* won a Regional Emmy Award in 2014. Kudos go to Mik Derks, who produced and edited the hour-long show. At this writing, my daughter, Susan, and I are working with PBS Wisconsin on my sixth hour-long documentary, this one based on our *Old Farm Country Cookbook*.

As a direct result of the success of the TV documentaries, the turnout at my book talks and book signings increased substantially, often doubling what I had been accustomed to. For instance, in early February 2014, I was asked to speak about my Wisconsin Historical Society Press book *Garden Wisdom* at the annual Landscape & Garden Expo at the Alliant Center in Madison. Attendance was 462, with people turned away because of the fire code. It was one of the largest audiences I had spoken to since I became a full-time writer in 1996. Many of those attending commented that they had seen one of my TV shows and wanted to talk with me. After my presentation, I signed books in the Wisconsin Historical Society Press booth, where they sold a record 260 copies of my books.

In 2013, I did a forty-five-minute PBS Wisconsin show where I answered questions about my experience with polio, which I had written about in my book *Limping through Life*, published that year by the WHS Press. As Rotary International has a longtime interest in helping to combat polio, I had received several requests from Rotary clubs to talk about my book. A recording of this TV show, sent free to clubs requesting it, helped me meet those requests without having to appear in person. *Limping through Life* was also the topic of a forty-five-minute

Ruth and I have chatted with thousands of people over the years at the annual Garden Expo in Madison. It seems that people who love to garden also love to read.

interview I did with Book TV on C-Span, broadcast nationally. I suspect that of all the marketing approaches I have used, television has helped me reach the most people.

One thing I learned early in my writing career: reaching people was just as important to me as writing a quality product. I also learned that there are many ways of doing so, from TV and radio shows to library talks, from Facebook Live to Zoom presentations, from bookstore signings to appearances at gift shops—and answering many, many emails.

Epilogue

Awards and Rewards

Awards weren't something I thought much about when I began writing professionally; my first book, *The Land Still Lives*, published in 1970, garnered several positive reviews but no awards. It was seven years later that I received my first award for a book, when *Barns of Wisconsin* received the Council for Wisconsin Writers' first-place award for nonfiction book writing. I was elated. For the first time, beyond reviews and positive comments from readers, I had affirmation from my writer peers that my writing had merit. I didn't mention this to anyone, but that single award gave me the psychological validation to continue writing. Since then, my books have received several awards and honors; in the sidebar, I've listed the ones that have meant the most to me.

I was anxious and uncertain when my first novel, *The Travels of Increase Joseph*, was published in 2003. Would anyone read it? My readers saw me as a nonfiction writer. Could I really cross genres successfully? By that time I had written six nonfiction trade books and fourteen academic books, but I had long wanted to add fiction to my

AWARDS MOST APPRECIATED

- First Place Award, Nonfiction Book, 1977, *Barns of Wisconsin*, Council for Wisconsin Writers (my first book award)
- Award of Merit for Distinguished Service to History, 1978, 1981, 1993, 1999, and 2003, Wisconsin Historical Society
- Outstanding Literary Achievement Award, 1993, Wisconsin Library Association
- Wisconsin Idea Award, 1994, University of Wisconsin Extension
- Award for Excellence in Interpretation of Wisconsin and Midwest Heritage, 1996
- Major Achievement Award, 2007, Council for Wisconsin Writers
- Notable Authors Award, 2007, Wisconsin Library Association
- Finalist in General Fiction, *Blue Shadows Farm* (2009) and *Cranberry Red* (2010), Midwest Book Awards (my first awards for fiction writing)
- Distinguished Service Award, 2010, College of Agricultural and Life Sciences, University of Wisconsin–Madison
- Elected as Fellow, 2012, Wisconsin Academy of Sciences, Arts, and Letters
- Regional Emmy Award, 2014, *A Farm Winter with Jerry Apps*
- White Cedar Outstanding Teaching Award, 2016, The Clearing Folk School

portfolio. One of my writer colleagues warned me when he heard that I had just published a novel, asking, "Do you want to be known as a nonfiction writer or a novelist?"

I wanted to answer (but didn't): "How about being known for both?"

I've also written children's picture books, young adult nonfiction books, and young adult novels. How do I want to be known, as a writer of adult nonfiction, adult fiction, children's picture books, young adult nonfiction, or young adult fiction? Again, my answer—never spoken aloud, and written here for the first time: "Why does a writer have to be pigeonholed to writing one type of book?" I understand the publishers' marketing challenges when an author writes in several genres. But after more than fifty years of writing books, what I am doing is working. Would I have done better sticking to adult nonfiction books? Or novels? Or children's and young adult books? Perhaps. But I will never know.

It would not be true for me to say awards haven't made a difference in my writing career. I enjoyed receiving them and appreciated when someone thought my work was of sufficient merit to honor it. But the rewards I have gotten in the form of comments from people who have read my books and watched my PBS documentaries have touched me beyond anything I could ever have imagined. Many times I have been stopped in hardware stores, grocery stores, restaurants, and parking lots with, "You're Jerry Apps, aren't you?"

"Yes," I answer.

"Well, I want you to know that my family really enjoys your books and your TV shows."

Talking with readers of all ages is the best reward of a writing life.

"Thank you," I say, even though I might be in the middle of searching for just the right bratwurst at the grocery store or out to dinner with my wife.

I receive many emails from people who have read my books or watched my PBS documentaries. Many say that I was telling their story, that what I have written or said has evoked memories long forgotten. Comments that have resonated the most are those telling me how when one of my TV documentaries aired, the entire family—grandparents, parents, and children—gathered to watch. "We want our grandkids to know what life on the farm was like when we were kids" is a comment I've heard often.

Such comments have been an important influence on my continuing to write during the autumn years of my life, when some of my friends and relatives believe I should spend more time enjoying my retirement. These twenty-five-plus years that I have been writing full-time have been some of the most fulfilling years of my life.

People ask me, "Why are you still writing? Aren't you supposed to be retired?" I sometimes facetiously answer, "I'm still learning how to do it. If I figure it out one day, I'll probably quit."

I enjoy many of the things thought to be part of retirement. Ruth and I spend time with our kids, grandchildren, and great-grandchildren as we celebrate birthdays and anniversaries and gather for a week at a lake every summer. When we are all together, the group numbers in the twenties. Ruth and I also spend many days at our farm, Roshara, every year. Until recently, we traveled often and spent a few weeks every year enjoying a Florida beach and warm temperatures. My retirement years have not been entirely consumed by writing.

Nevertheless, I've gained much from this life in writing. Now and again someone hints that because I have written a number of books and have done several television documentaries, I must be rolling in cash. For the Wisconsin Public Television projects, I donated my time, no payment. Public television is one of this country's treasures, and I was more than pleased to contribute my time and ideas. The money I have made from writing books has been modest—enough to help my grandkids earn college degrees without student loans. I am more than a little proud that I have been able to do this.

But what I have gained from writing goes far beyond the monetary. As a shy farm kid recovering from polio, writing helped me come out from behind myself. When I was unable to play sports and do what other kids my age were doing, writing helped me combat my feelings of worthlessness—a lingering psychological effect of polio. I am so thankful for high school teachers who pointed me toward becoming a member of the school's newspaper staff, where I eventually became the editor. There I discovered not only some of the skills needed for writing but the joy of accomplishment—I had found something that I could do and something that others appreciated. It gave my life an added purpose.

Writing helped me learn things I never thought I would learn, travel to places I never thought I would visit, meet people I never thought I would encounter, and do things I thought I would never do. Writing taught me to listen for the whispers and look in the shadows. Listen to the quiet sounds amidst a world of shouting, look in the shadows where the bright light doesn't shine—and discover things often overlooked.

Writing has helped me learn how to accept rejection and move on. I have learned that there will always be writers who are better than I am. The sense that my writing is viewed as having value—helping evoke memories, applauding the values and beliefs of farm life, and supporting a concern for the environment—is another important reason—perhaps the most important reason—that I continue to write.

I am reminded of something I wrote in my journal on October 1, 1999: "I had a strange feeling the other day. I sensed old age circling above me like a hawk fixing to pounce on a field mouse. When I am creating things, writing or speaking, this 'old age hawk' disappears. Now, as I am writing, no hawk circles overhead. Weird."

When I wrote that, I was sixty-five years old. At this writing, I am twenty-two years older. But I still find writing soothing, stress relieving, a way to take my mind off the worrisome things those of us labeled "elderly" regularly face.

Sometimes, as I'm writing, I wonder if anyone cares—that is, until I get an email like the one I recently received from a young farm woman who lives in northeastern Wisconsin. She said that her husband had been seriously injured in a farm accident and couldn't work for many weeks. She wrote, "I was afraid my husband was going to commit suicide, and I didn't know what to do." What she did was visit her local library and ask if they had any books that might help her husband. The librarian sent her home with a couple of my books. "You helped save my husband's life," she wrote. I believe she was being overly generous with her comment, but her email surely touched me.

Not long after that, another young woman emailed me. She wrote, "My father, a longtime farmer, died last week. He was a great fan of your books. I wanted you to know that he asked me, when he was dying, to read from one of your books. I did this. Thank you."

During the COVID-19 epidemic in 2020–2021, I received this in an email:

> As the world has been forced to slow down during these awful circumstances, so many people I know are having their eyes opened to the beauty of this land, and just how much they have been rushing through life, not even taking the time to see the world around them. . . . It's been less of a startling transition for me, and that is greatly in part because I picked up your book this past winter. It has helped me immensely embrace the time that I am in. Even if it's difficult, slow, cold and dark. Even if things feel uncertain.

Letters and emails like this keep me writing.

Appendix

Published Books

BOOKS RELATED TO RURAL HISTORY AND RURAL LIFE

The Land Still Lives. Wisconsin House, 1970. Wisconsin Historical Society Press, 2019.

Cabin in the Country. Argus, 1973.

Village of Roses. Wild Rose Historical Society, 1973.

Barns of Wisconsin. Wisconsin Trails, 1977, 1995. Wisconsin Historical Society Press, 2010.

Mills of Wisconsin and the Midwest. Wisconsin Trails, 1980.

Skiing into Wisconsin. Pearl Win Publications, 1985.

Breweries of Wisconsin. University of Wisconsin Press, 1992, 2005.

One-Room Country Schools. Amherst Press, 1996. Wisconsin Historical Society Press, 2015.

Wisconsin Traveler's Companion. Wisconsin Trails, 1997. (Out of print)

Rural Wisdom. Amherst Press, 1997. (Out of print)

Cheese: The Making of a Wisconsin Tradition. Amherst Press, 1998. Second Edition, University of Wisconsin Press, 2020.

When Chores Were Done. Amherst Press, 1999. Voyageur Press, 2006.

Symbols: Viewing a Rural Past. Amherst Press, 2000. Republished as *Country Ways and Country Days*, Voyageur Press, 2005.

Humor from the Country. Amherst Press, 2001. Voyageur Press, 2006.

The People Came First: A History of Wisconsin Cooperative Extension. Cooperative Extension Publications, 2002.

Eat Rutabagas. Amherst Press, 2002.

Stormy. Amherst Press, 2002.

The Travels of Increase Joseph. Badger Books, 2003. University of Wisconsin Press, 2010.

Ringlingville USA. Wisconsin Historical Society Press, 2004.

Every Farm Tells a Story. Voyageur Press, 2005. Wisconsin Historical Society Press, 2018.

Country Ways and Country Days. Voyageur Press. 2005.

Country Wisdom. Voyageur Press, 2005.

Tents, Tigers, and the Ringling Brothers. Wisconsin Historical Society Press, 2006.

Living a Country Year. Voyageur Press, 2007. Wisconsin Historical Society Press, 2018.

In a Pickle: A Family Farm Story. University of Wisconsin Press, 2007.

Casper Jaggi: Master Swiss Cheese Maker. Wisconsin Historical Society Press, 2008.

Old Farm: A History. Wisconsin Historical Society Press, 2008.

Blue Shadows Farm. University of Wisconsin Press, 2009.

Horse-Drawn Days: A Century of Farming with Horses. Wisconsin Historical Society Press, 2010.

Cranberry Red. University of Wisconsin Press, 2010.

Campfires and Loon Calls. Fulcrum Publishing, 2011.

Garden Wisdom: Lessons Learned from 60 Years of Gardening. Wisconsin Historical Society Press, 2012.

Rural Wit and Wisdom. Fulcrum Press, 2012.

Tamarack River Ghost. University of Wisconsin Press, 2012.

Letters from Hillside Farm. Fulcrum Press, 2013.

The Quiet Season. Wisconsin Historical Society Press, 2013.

Limping through Life: A Farm Boy's Polio Memoir. Wisconsin Historical Society Press, 2013.

The Great Sand Fracas of Ames County. University of Wisconsin Press, 2014.

Whispers and Shadows. Wisconsin Historical Society Press, 2015.

Wisconsin Agriculture: A History. Wisconsin Historical Society Press, 2015.

Telling Your Story. Fulcrum Press, 2016.

Roshara Journal: Chronicling Four Seasons, Fifty Years, and 120 Acres. Wisconsin Historical Society Press, 2016.

Never Curse the Rain. Wisconsin Historical Society Press, 2017.

Old Farm Country Cookbook. With Susan Apps-Bodilly. Wisconsin Historical Society Press, 2017.

Cold as Thunder. University of Wisconsin Press, 2018.

Once a Professor: A Memoir of Teaching in Turbulent Times. Wisconsin Historical Society Press, 2018.

Simple Things: Lessons from the Family Farm. Wisconsin Historical Society Press, 2018.

The Civilian Conservation Corps in Wisconsin: Nature's Army at Work. Wisconsin Historical Society Press, 2019.

When the White Pine Was King. Wisconsin Historical Society Press, 2020.

The Old Timer Says: A Writing Journal. Wisconsin Historical Society Press, 2020.

Settlers Valley. University of Wisconsin Press, 2021.

The Wild Oak. Three Towers Press, 2021.

Meet Me on the Midway: A History of Wisconsin Fairs. Wisconsin Historical Society Press, 2022.

More Than Words: A Memoir of a Writing Life. Wisconsin Historical Society Press, 2022.

BOOKS RELATED TO EDUCATION

How to Improve Adult Education in Your Church. Augsburg, 1972.

Toward a Working Philosophy of Adult Education. Syracuse University Press, 1973.

Tips for Article Writers. Wisconsin Regional Writers, 1973.

Ideas for Better Church Meetings. Augsburg, 1975.

Study Skills for Adults Returning to School. McGraw-Hill, 1978, 1981.

Problems in Continuing Education. McGraw-Hill, 1980. Spanish translation, Paidos Educador, Barcelona, 1983, 1994.

The Adult Learner on Campus. Follett, 1981.

Improving Your Writing Skills. Follett, 1982.

Improving Practice in Continuing Education. Jossey-Bass, 1985.

Higher Education in a Learning Society. Jossey-Bass, 1988.

Study Skills for Today's College Student. McGraw-Hill, 1990.

Mastering the Teaching of Adults. Krieger, 1991.

Higher Education in a Learning Society. Arabic translation. Dar Al-bashir, Amman, Jordon, 1991.

Leadership for the Emerging Age. Jossey-Bass, 1994.

Teaching from the Heart. Krieger, 1996.

Acknowledgments

So many people should be acknowledged for helping me to start and keep my writing career alive over these fifty-five years that I have been writing professionally. First, I must credit my wife, Ruth, who reads everything I write and offers both criticism and praise. If Ruth says no to a piece of my writing, it goes on the "not to be published" shelf in my office.

I have worked with scores of editors over the years, none more professional or capable than Kate Thompson, who is the director of the Wisconsin Historical Society Press. Kate knows how to push me to write beyond what I think I am capable of doing, all with a friendly smile. She and I have worked together on many books; I so appreciate all that she has done. Kristin Gilpatrick, sales and marketing manager, and Chris Caldwell, events coordinator, also with the Wisconsin Historical Society Press, have been invaluable in getting the word out about my books.

My daughter, Sue Apps-Bodilly, deserves special recognition. We have written books together and now are creating a TV documentary together. Sue, a second-grade teacher, is especially helpful with the books I write for young readers. My daughter-in-law Natasha Kassulke and I are writing a book together as well. With a journalism and science background, she is a wonderfully competent writer and editor and has produced short internet promotional pieces about my books. My son Steve, a photojournalist and documentary photographer, has paired up with me on several book projects and has helped me with several novels. My son Jeff, a financial counselor in Colorado, gives a good informed layperson read of my draft material. A big thank you to my nephew Matt Apps, a computer whiz, who helped create my website and currently serves as my webmaster. He also helped me become a Facebook member and steered me into blog writing.

A special thank you to Robert Gard, now deceased, who served as my writing mentor in the early years of my writing career and published my first book, *The Land Still Lives*.

To all the bookstores, public libraries, local historical societies, farm organizations, and other groups that have invited me to speak: thank you. You have helped introduce my books to readers. Thanks to farm publication editors James Massey, who was editor of *The Country Today* and ran my columns for several years; Colleen Kottke, editor of the *Wisconsin State Farmer*, who publishes my blog as a weekly column; Julie Belschner, editor of *Agri-View*, who ran my columns at one time; and Fran O'Leary, editor of the *Wisconsin Agriculturist*, who has long supported my work.

To Larry Meiller of the *Larry Meiller Show* on Wisconsin Public Radio, a huge thank you. I have been on Larry's radio show many times over the years promoting my books. And thank you to Pam Jahnke of the *Midwest Farm Report*. I have done a number of radio shows with her as well. I thank Jon Miskowski, director of PBS Wisconsin, for his support and encouragement as I was featured in five hour-long documentaries. Special thanks to Mik Derks, who so ably directed those shows.

Thank you to Marv Balousek, one-time owner of Badger Books, for taking a chance when he published my first novel, *The Travels of Increase Joseph*. I also want to thank all the small and midsized publishers that have published my books over the years—more than twenty of them.

I doubt my writing would ever have gotten started if it had not been for the encouragement of two of my high school teachers, Paul Wright and Bill Harvey. Those teachers saw something in me that I didn't see in myself.

And finally, I cannot say thank you enough to the many thousands of readers who have purchased my books and watched my TV shows. A writer without readers is like a car without tires. Neither one is going very far.

About the Author

Jerry Apps was born and raised on a central Wisconsin farm. He is a former county extension agent and professor emeritus for the College of Agriculture and Life Sciences at the University of Wisconsin–Madison. Today he works as a rural historian, full-time writer, and creative writing instructor. Jerry is the author of more than fifty fiction, nonfiction, and children's books, many of them on rural history, country life, and storytelling. His work has won awards from the American Library Association, the Wisconsin Library Association, the Wisconsin Historical Society, and the Council for Wisconsin Writers, and he has created six hour-long documentaries about farm life and country living with PBS Wisconsin. He and his wife, Ruth, divide their time between their home in Madison and their farm, Roshara, in Waushara County.